Simply Inspirational Speaking

Karen North

4

The right of Karen North to be identified as the
Author of the Work has been asserted by them in accordance
with the Copyright, Designs and Patents Act 1988.

Copyright © Karen North 2020

Simply Inspirational Speaking

Printed and bound in the UK by
4edge, 22 Eldon Way, Hockley, Essex, SS5 4AD

ISBN: 978-1-913637-02-6

Published by
Candy Jar Books
Mackintosh House
136 Newport Road, Cardiff, CF24 1DJ
www.candyjarbooks.co.uk

To my friend
Adrienne,
a truly spiritual lady,
who always supports me
and has encouraged me to compile this book.
Thank you so much, your friendship means everything to me.
Karen

Contents

Preface
Spiritualism

S Speak the truth that death is nothing at all.
P Place trust in yourself for you are spirit here and now.
I Immerse yourself in the concept of a spiritual life.
R Respect the power of love that is from God the Father.
I Investigate the gifts of the spirit within you.
T Think positively throughout the challenges of life.
U Utilise the power within you to be of service to others.
A Acknowledge the sensitivity of your own spirit.
L Listen to the 'still small voice' from within.
I Involve yourself in a full life, for life is for living.
S Slowly build on your understanding that life is eternal.
M Muster strength to live by that truth and share it.

Chapter One
Barry Spirtualists' National Union (SNU) Church, Buttrills Road, Barry

SUNDAY 23RD MARCH 2014

GOOD EVENING to you, my friends, it is a pleasure to come and to talk with you.

Because, you know, we in the spirit world have much to say to you on the earth plane, because many of you are willing to listen to what we have to say to put a different idea forward from time to time, because, you know, in your day to day living you become enmeshed within materialism, within the material physical world, because you see you are journeying forward in that world and your spiritual self is journeying with you because it is the spirit that is encased within that physical form.

And so, when you reach that point in your life that you call death, it is but shedding the overcoat of the physical body and setting free your true self. That spirit, that is you. The real person that you are. And then, with that spirit being released from the confines of the physical body and matter of your world, then a new life begins. And so, it is that there is the continuance of the spirit, and it is one of your principles, is it not? That the spirit continues into that world of light.

And that poem that was read was chosen by a lady that was not particularly interested in your religion of Spiritualism, and yet that was a poem that told you that life continued and that you were not to grieve and shed tears. You were to help that person on their continuing journey of life by remembering the love shown to you, and to remember that you also showed love to that individual, and that is how it is, your life with your family and your friends.

You may, indeed, have disagreement from time to time, because that is inevitable, you know, because sometimes you have to air your grievances and clear the air because you are all individuals with different ideas and ideals and different problems that you face throughout your life's span. And so, you learn, shall we say, the art of compromise and you have to give and to take.

And so, it is in our world also. All of you can be channels for the spirit in your day to day living. Because the gifts of the spirit are bestowed on all of you. No one is exempt from the gifts of the spirit, because the spirit is the real person that you are. So you all have ability, you see, to help yourself firstly and in so doing to help others. And so, there is this give and take from one state of existence to another; that is why we in the spirit world are so interested in what you get up to in your life. You are all seeking understanding of the spirit of the truth, of the journey that you are undertaking and the journey that will continue as you transform that spirit within you from one state existence to another.

In your world there is much that will worry you and

the world as a whole that you see through your media channels is a little daunting to say the least. Because it seems that one person always seems to be fighting another. Not just in your war-torn countries, but individuals also can clash quite heavily with each other.

But we would tell to you that the light of the spirit is always at hand to guide and assist you, the individual. If the individual can find peace within themselves and everybody tried to do that, then your world would soon calm itself down and you would see how it is that the light of the spirit can dwell amongst mankind in your earthly existence of life.

There have been many that have walked the earth shining that light of their own spirit and working with those guides and helpers from the spiritual realms, and much has been documented when they are promoting all of the time, peace and love to be shared one with the other.

It is a case, you know, of understanding what that spirit within you is. And understanding that, although you grieve the loss of the physical of your loved ones, their spirit continues, and they are very much aware of you living within the earth's vibration.

And so, nothing is lost and there is much to gain by linking with that spirit within and the spirit world. You are asked that you test the spirit, because much information is imparted to you, on an individual basis, through your own mind, through the dream state, and yet you push it aside sometimes without any thought, telling yourself that you have a vivid imagination or the dream was nonsense or the fact that you just might be dealing with coincidence. But we would say to you, that all this that you think and put aside in those ways is really what we would term reality.

For your life on the earth can be one of illusion, if you do not get down to the nitty gritty of understanding yourself as a spiritual individual, as a being of light, the light to be shone forth in your actions. Because sometimes words can be empty, you know, and yet your actions will speak volumes to many. And so, you have to go about your business with the correct motives so that you are being honest with yourself. And then you see your gifts of the spirit will come to the fore.

You all have feelings, do you not? You may be house hunting to change your place of abode, and you would know instantly, as you stepped across the threshold of the property, whether it was for you or not, because you are sensitive of the vibrations of the spirit world and of the physical world also. And so you have to be passionate about what you want, and if you can work with that passion in your day to day living, then your life will be, indeed, a lot easier as you move forward.

Too many of you put obstacles in your way that need not be there because your mind goes off on a tangent and you fear the worse outcome possible, and so your mind is in what we would term overdrive. That is why it is good if you can find time in your day to rest your mind, and although meditation may seem difficult, you know, you all daydream from time to time, even with your eyes open. How many of you have been driving a vehicle and then realised that you've not remembered how you got to those set of traffic lights and you missed the roundabout in between? But you are driving on automatic pilot, shall we say, and then you see you

4

forget what you have seen.

And so it is in the way that we can work with you; if you allow yourself to have an open mind then we can influence you for the better, to give you these good ideas as to a way forward, around and over the obstacles that you all have to face in day to day living.

And so, you know, those words of that poem were telling you about an afterlife, because it ended by saying that you would be welcomed home by that individual that you would have been grieving over, at the loss. And so, they were quite adamant that they were going to travel into a different life, and so it is that we want to give you all this hope and this understanding of the continuous existence of the human soul.

It is important that people understand this truth and want to ask questions and find out for themselves by having proof of survival of the spirit of their loved ones and friends. And so it is good for you to keep inquiring minds and asking questions, because we in the spirit world do not get tired of those questions, so you see when you say your prayers you are linking with the spirit world, and it is not always please can I have this, that or the other, because you all have concerns for your world as a whole and you know that there is much that is needed to bring healing to your planet, for the kingdom or nature and animals, and for everything that is about in your world.

Because there is a power, a power that you know to be the Fatherhood of God, that keeps things in an orderly fashion, but there are many in your world that try to take control; you cannot have power over God, but you can work within the power of the Great Spirit of God the Father.

You all have, in equal measure, the same spirit and God power within you. It is up to you how you use it and utilise it in your best interests and in the best interests of those that walk with you from the spirit realms of life. And so, we would remind you of your personal responsibility in your own way of living. Look towards the light of God the Father and you cannot fail in your quest. You will automatically move on, your spirit will be free, at some time, from the confines of matter. And then you will see the beauty of the spirit world and the purpose of your life for a short time that was spent in physical matter. And so you see you are all journeying on the same journey of life, and so we wish you well, my friends, in that journey, and we promise to give you all the help that you need, and all that we need you to do is to accept the truth that there is no death only eternal life.

And so, we say to you, my friends, good night and God bless.

SUNDAY 10TH MAY 2015

GOOD EVENING to you, my friends, it is a pleasure to come and to talk with you.

And to, indeed, lift your spirits so that you can, indeed, move mountains in your daily day to day routines, that can be burdensome to say the least, because, you know, it's so easy to get into a comfortable rut, shall we say. But you know the power within you, the spirit, is always alive and well and working towards the time when your own transition will occur, and you will have reached that state that you call death that we call rebirth.

And so, it is important that you do understand the power that you have within yourself to remove obstacles that may be in your way, that will raise you up over difficulties, just as you have sung. It is important, therefore, that we understand all about the continuous existence of the human soul, and as difficult as it may be when you lose loved ones and they move on, on their soul journey, you are despairing of that loss, because that is part of you as a human being. It is part of your human nature, just as it is that you are looking for answers to questions, for you are going to want to go and look and see further than you can with those physical eyes, with your mind. Your spirit within is prompting you in the direction that is right for you.

Some may never want to come into a building such as this, and yet they may be spiritually enlightened, using their power and their energy to aid others who appear to be less fortunate than themselves. For each one of us has needs, and we must, to a certain extent, rely on others to help us along life's journey. It is not a journey that we make alone, for there are those in the spirit world that join us, that help us, albeit that they are unseen and may remain unseen, until you meet again in the spiritual realms of life.

It's important, therefore, that you are willing to take responsibility in your life, to do the best that you can do under the given circumstances that you find yourself in. You know, we have to accept many things in the physical world that we feel are unjust and unfair, and we must look for the common good. We have to look to see what is best for us, the individual, so that we may come to terms with what it is we have to do, so that we have a fulfilling life. As long as you look within yourselves and you find your passion, then you are along the right road for unfolding your spiritual gifts. For the gifts of the spirit are many, and you know, just to give a helping hand or a lovely smile can aid another. For we never really understand anyone else's pathway in life. We may be able to sympathise and empathise, but we are well and truly living our own life in our own shoes. We can support, we can uphold, but we cannot control or live the life of someone else. We have to be true to ourselves.

And so, there is that principle within Spiritualism of Personal Responsibility. Because it is our responsibility to do our best, to help ourselves and in so doing to help others. You may look into a mirror and think that you do not like what you see, but what you see is the physical body only; you do not see your true spiritual essence. The spirit world, and those that walk with you in that realm of life, see the spirit that you are, the soul that you are, and they know what it is that you are learning along

8

life's way. So, be proud of your accomplishments, because even to be a good homemaker, to be a good provider, in itself is an accolade that you can be proud of. To make something a comfortable experience is what is asked of each one of you. When power is misaligned or misused then you are going to feel uncomfortable in that place or in that relationship, and so you have then to look at what you think is the problem. And you know, even when there are problems within your world, there are many that can aid you outside of your close family and friends.

And so, you see there is a network building up that ensures that you can indeed better your life, better your understanding and better yourself. Nothing at all is insurmountable when you look to God, the Creator of life. Those in the spirit world are willing to guide and help you along the way, and that is part and parcel of the continuous existence of the human soul, another principle that we have mentioned earlier.

And so, you see in those seven principles you are able to find that you can interpret them in such a way that you are able to help yourself in your understanding of spiritual truths. Those were given through the mediumship of Emma Hardinge Britten, and she was able to set them forth to be the backbone of the religion known as Spiritualism. So, be brave and take hold of that power that is within you and move forward in your life. Stand up, allow the power to raise you up so that you can help others that need a little guidance in the understanding that they are not just on this earth and then at a certain time they will die, and that will be the end. It is but the beginning of a new life. That is indeed the great power of the Creator, of the Great Spirit. It does not matter what religions tell you.

You have to just be confident within yourself. There are no creeds or dogmas within Spiritualism; you are allowed free thinking, for you are a free spirit. The only confines that your spirit has, at this time, is the confines of your own physical body. There are many that would wish to talk to you through the communication from the spirit world, and can do so within your dream state within those times when you consider that you are daydreaming, but when your mind is a little less active they can help you. They can inspire you; they can move you forward. So be brave and acknowledge your communication within your own self that comes from the spirit world. You all have what you term intuition, and when you go against what you know to be right, then you have a little trouble in moving along that pathway.

The material and the spiritual pathways should run parallel, you see, and then you will feel fulfilled within your own being, within your own life, and you will know that nothing can destruct you, for the spirit is the spirit and the physical is the physical. You are just wearing what you may term an overcoat, and then the spirit will have its freedom when it returns to that world of light and love. So, go forward in that knowledge and understanding of the powerful being that you are. Use your power wisely and you cannot fail. Be true to yourself. Always ask questions and you find answers, and then you can indeed be counted as a good and faithful servant of the spirit. You will understand more when you move back into that world of the spirit, and you will see that your work has been good and that is all that we ask of you, my friends, is that you do what is right for you and in so doing aid others. Bring forward that light of understanding that there is no death only eternal life.

And we say to you, my friends, good night and God bless.

Chapter Two

Bridgend SNU Church, The Rhiw, Bridgend

SUNDAY 18TH MAY 2014

GOOD EVENING to you, my friends, it is a pleasure to come and to talk with you.

And what shall we say, to bring into your midst the power of the spirit that is within you. Because you all contribute to the energy that is within this room, because you are all living and vibrant, and your spirit, believe it or believe it not, is alive and well. You may not feel alive and well, but your spirit is alive and well.

And so, it is that you are journeying through your life in the material world, and that is part of the journey that you have to make before your spirit leaves the confines of matter, the confines of the physical body, that you term you. But we would say to you that the real person that you are, the essence of you, is the spirit within you, and that power drives you through your life's work, within the material world.

It is good when you all come together so that the power of the spirit can build, and then you have what you term communication with the spirit world. And so, it is that you can find that power within yourself, and that is good. That is why you can sit within your circles so that you can develop your spiritual gifts, but more importantly develop your spirituality, so that you then want to be a channel to serve others with the help and the aid of the guides and helpers that link with your spirit, with your soul, so that you can evolve through your life and you can begin to question what is beyond the confines of matter.

You have sung about the beacon of light that is going to help all those that are in need. And so it is that the spirit world is always there with you; whether you perceive that or not, it can be irrelevant, but you know when you open your heart and your mind to the fact that the spirit world are with you twenty four seven, then you can get to grips with what life is all about.

It does not make sense if you were just to die and there be nothing beyond the earthly vibration. It would not make sense. Many people within your world do not want to investigate what may be beyond the confines of matter. And they are the ones that need your help and assistance and your aid. Because sometimes, you know, just listening to somebody that is having trouble in their lives helps a great deal. And when they can see how calm that you are with your understanding of the fact that life is eternal, then they see; they are inspired by action, you see. And all of you can act upon your understanding of your own spiritual self. And so, there are many questions to be asked and many answers to be given, but you see, you have to have what we would term an open mind.

You may complain that in your life there are many trials and tribulations for you to face and overcome. But in all that striving forward, your spirit is moving forward, so that you become a stronger person within yourself. So that you then begin to ask your questions and seek your answers. So, we want you all to feel enthused and to feel positive about your life in the material world, because you are all giving but not many wish to receive.

And when you work for the spirit world then you have to have this ebb and flow of giving of yourself and receiving from the spiritual realms of life so that the circle is forever moving forward. Because we cannot expect of you that you give of yourself until you are exhausted, and that is why it is so important to understand the fifth principle within your Spiritualism of Personal Responsibility.

You have had those principles read out to you, and you know they are open to your own interpretation, but we say to you if you look at them one by one and ask questions you will begin to receive many answers, because there are many things that can be interpreted in a different way, and so it is that you can expand your understanding and in so doing expand your Spiritualism out into the world.

The wider world because when you understand that there is Eternal Progress open to every Human Soul, then you can see how the spirit world has much work to do to get people to be prompted by their own spirit. You know, sometimes you judge a book by its cover, so to speak, and you may think as you look at our channel here this evening that she is a little bit, what shall we say, incapacitated, but you know that does not mean that she cannot link with the spirit world and bring forward our message.

Because, you know, sometimes you want to give aid and help, and you know, sometimes it is not required because of the spirit being so strong. And so it is with the individual that you are: when you need that help from the spirit most of all, it may be when your physical body is the most robust, the most healthy. But some people will not look within until that physical body is failing in some way or another. That is why your healers are so important as channels for the spirit world, because too many come in through that door and look to healing as the last resort and not the first.

But, you know, things have turned around for many who have had a frail and ailing physical body, and then that proves the power of the spirit within and the power of the spirit that is channelled through others. And so, we want that light to shine brightly, as that hymn said, so that all may follow in the light of the spirit, in the light of God the Father.

And you know, all of you of the human race are of the same essence that of spirit, and so that makes you all in the terms of your principles a brotherhood. You are all equal, you see, within that physical being that you are, irrespective of how the body works, irrespective of what colour that body may be or what encumberment it may have to push you forward on your correct pathway of spiritual understanding. And that is what your life in this physical world is all about: it's about understanding yourselves. It is about understanding the laws of the spirit.

And so, that brings us to another one of your principles: compensation and retribution for all the good and not so good deeds done on earth. You are in charge, my friends, of you. We only come as close as you allow to aid you and assist you in your journey. So it is important that you also understand about the communion of spirits and the ministry of angels, because what you term miracles happen in your world. Do not be fobbed off by these people that can explain all things to you. There is many a mystery to be solved, you know, so you can all go around, if you like, as Clouseau or Miss Marple and investigate in your own way, because that is good, that is moving the mind forward. That is moving the spirit within you so that you can begin to work in the way of God the Father.

Looking towards that light, that perfection, you even sang a hymn of 'All Things Bright and Beautiful', and all that encompasses the power of the spirit, because your world has its seasons come what may. You may not always be able to distinguish between summer and winter because of what you term global warming, but you know it can be cold in summer and warm in winter. It can be dry in winter and raining in summer. It all seems topsy turvy to you sometimes, but nevertheless the seasons continue, your world exists within that great universe, and so it is that you are you, and we want you to understand that you can always be sure of the truth that your spirit will transcend and transform at that time that you call death. And so, we want you to take that understanding forward, we want you to commit to that power of the spirit so that your Spiritualism can grow, can grow within your church, can grow within your community, can grow within your world.

So, that responsibility that is yours, and just, what

shall we say, concentrate on yourself finding peace within your very being and do you know, when you can do that you will find that peace will transcend into your world from ours. Because we can make that peace, the bridge between one state of existence and the other. They are always joined together, my friends, but we need you, all of you, to be channels for those that would wish to come forward to prove the power of the spirit to others that are doubtful, that are negative, and so we want you to be joyful and positive and in so doing then you will see transformation within your world. You will not have to worry, quite so much, because your media always brings to you the bad news of the day. They never ever bring to you the good news of the day. And so, we say to you, my friends, indeed walk in that light, in the light of God the Father, that is love eternal.

And we say to you, my friends, good night and God bless.

SUNDAY 21ST SEPTEMBER 2014

GOOD EVENING to you, my friends, it is a pleasure to come and to talk with you even if you put a time limit in place, it does not matter to us, in our world, because we like to work around the constraints of your world time is something that constrains you all, because, you know, you feel from time to time that time is running out. You have this to do and that do, and it doesn't seem that you have enough time to get it all done.

But we chose that reading this evening to give to you because there is so much in your world that seems to be of disharmony, and there seems to be people fighting people in the name of religion. That has been the case for eons of time, and you know you only have to press a button to get on to your TV or on to your internet to find more and more discontent and disharmony within your world, and that causes us, in our world, much distress, you know.

And so, we understand that you, as human beings, are also distressed by many things that you see and many things that you have to become involved in in your life, when you are searching for answers to questions. Because life does not make sense, at all, if it just ends at that point that you call death, at that point that we call rebirth. Because that is what happens when your spirit is no longer encased in the physical form and is no longer part of the material world. And that is when, you see, we can see you, in your true colours.

And it will not matter one jot as to what religion you followed. It will all revolve around what you did in your life. What you did to help yourself, and what you did to help others. It is simple, but you in your world, the human race make it so complicated that sometimes you will fail to understand why one person is fighting another to gain power over others, in your world of matter.

It is a little disconcerting for us, but we never give up to bring you the message, the message about life being eternal, you know. It is not going to end at that point that you call death, but of course, you are going to miss the physical presence of your loved ones and friends that you have spent many a long time helping. In your family life you help one another, some families do not help each other but they still at one point have lived together.

And so, you see, you are co-dependent, one upon another. Because that is what life is about in your world of the physical. It is very difficult for the message to come across, and do you know that, you know, in your churches, you know, they are sparse in number, your members, but that does not put us off giving out the message of the spirit, because we don't need you to wear labels and belong to a certain church. We want you to look within yourself for the gifts of the spirit. You have a very accomplished lady there that can play music for you and add a little bit of swing to your hymns, to your words, that you sing together, that you blend together in one voice and that is why we want you to blend together the spirit, that is why you begin by sending out your thoughts. You are all then focused on the point in question, which is to give of yourself and your energy to aid others. You don't have to stand up and be counted and wear a big banner saying that you are a Spiritualist, or that you belong to the religion of Spiritualism because that will not matter in our world.

You know, you despair, from time to time, at the war and fighting within your world and yet you only see the devastation of the war, you do not see all the work that is done with people giving of their own spirit, giving of their time, giving of their work within the medical field, as one example would be. And through those that give like that, then that aids your modern medicine, your modern technology, you know, because you see everybody is out to be of service to those that are less fortunate, depending on where they live. On your news you never hear, very often, good news, it's all not so good news, that can terrorise you into believing that the world is not a good place to be, but rest assured, my friends, it is a marvellous place to be, because while you are journeying within the physical world, then your soul is refining itself and you are making strides forward into becoming the true spirits that you are, the spirit that is about helping others, helping yourself. In your churches you administer healing, in your churches you prove survival of the spirit, in your churches you help one another, in your churches you tell the message. But how many people respond to what you are doing and what you are saying.

Each one of you has to take on board that fifth principle of Personal Responsibility. It is up to you to enlighten others when they question you about their fear, about their misunderstanding as to what happens when the spirit of their loved one, or friend, leaves the physical body. My friends, all of you, have communication with the spirit world in one way or another.

And so it is that you are to give out the message. It is important, therefore, that you do not just talk about religion and blame religion and religious beliefs for all the trouble within your world. Look deep within yourselves to find the power of the spirit; it is there, my friends, for each one of you. Nobody is exempt because you are all spirit, part of the great Creator that you call God, the Great Spirit of life. And so it is that we would put that to you, so that you can take on board your own responsibility for what you do, and maybe more importantly how you do it, because we want to give to you confidence, we want to give to you reassurance that your world is not a dark, dismal, uneventful place that only deals in destruction.

You started this service by talking about your weather and the beautiful day that you have had, because there is the kingdom of nature that provides all within your world. It can be a little difficult at times with storms, but you get nice days and not so nice days, and that is part and parcel of life within the physical world. And so, we would say to you, look at things in a positive manner, look at things in the light, do not dwell on the misery and darkness of your world. Things will work out, my friends, as long as you are doing what you should do and linking with that spirit within and those that work with you from the spirit world – friends, guides, helpers, it does not matter, because you are all one in the essence of the spirit that you are. And so take heed, take your religion seriously by all means, but it does not matter what rules or regulations are in place as long as you adhere to the spiritual laws of life, and that is in your principles also, as Compensation and

Retribution Hereafter for all the Good and Evil deeds done on Earth. That, my friends, are the guidelines that you work by, and when you return to the spirit you will be able to see what you have accomplished and how good those accomplishments have been, if you walk in the light of God the Creator and God the Father.

And so, we say to you, my friends, goodnight and God bless.

Chapter Three
Brunswick SNU Church, Kepple Place, Plymouth

SUNDAY 3RD JUNE 2012 (AFTERNOON SERVICE)
GOOD AFTERNOON to you. It is a pleasure to come and to talk with you and to give you a little bit of encouragement, because from time to time you become a little bit lazy with your thought processes, do you not? You forget about yourselves, you are always in constant worry mode, shall we say, for other people, and help is what you wish to give. And, indeed, to be of service to one another is working for the spirit. Because it is the spirit within that is going to impress upon you what is right and what is wrong, and as soon as you feel a little bit of discomfort, within the solar plexus area especially, then you will know that you are not quite on the track that is correct for you. And sometimes, you know, it only needs a word of kindness, or a smile to enable somebody else to feel uplifted.

For those of you who work in the healing sphere, it is not always the laying on of hands that is important, but you can send out healing through your mind and thought processes. Because, you know, it is very enlightening if you can have time to sit in the silence and, as you call it, meditate. It is important, you see, that you think that you have to put time aside for constant meditation, whereas in point of fact, you are always linking with the spirit world because your communication processes by thought; thoughts are so refined that sometimes you cannot choose which is your thought and which is there placed by those that walk with you from the spirit side of life.

How many times do you say, it is only imagination? We have news for you, your imagination is the tool that we can use to get you up and running and working well, for those in the spirit world and for your own spiritual progress as well.

And so, it is simplicity that we look for, you see. We don't want to over complicate matters, and these days many of you have over complicated lives, whereas all that you have to do is to ensure that you are thinking to do your best for yourself and for others, and then you cannot go wrong. What happens is that some people have what you may term a hidden agenda in their lives, and they are wanting to manipulate things to their advantage, rather than face up to what life has to offer for them.

Because, you see, it is that spirit that is going to sustain you through thick and thin. It is that spirit within you that is going to allow you to pass through that veil that you call death and arrive in the world of the spirit. It is no mystery. It is a natural occurrence that you all will, at some time, make your transition, so that the spirit is free from the confines of the physical body, and you are going to journey on. So, the more that you understand of your own thoughts and those of the spirit realms, the sooner you will be at peace with yourself.

Because, you see, it is important that you understand the power of the spirit and also the power of thought. You can talk yourself wonderfully into self, and you can do the same and talk yourself out of self, and you have to be very discerning as to what you want, because your wants are not always the same as your needs, and so it is that your needs are taken care of by that Great Creator that you call God. And sometimes your wants cannot be taken care of, but to know you are often inspired to do what is best at the best time for you. Because, of course, as your principles state, you have to take on board Personal Responsibility, and that is why it is important that you check your thoughts, that you do sit and think and allow your minds to wander, because it is all to do with states of awareness, and you know we are now speaking through our medium, with just a slight control.

Because, you see, there are varying degrees as to consciousness, and when you are in your physical body sometimes you do not allow your mind to take you on journeys where enlightenment can be gained.

There are many that are gurus in the Eastern religions that transcend into the spiritual realms, while their spirit is still within the body, and yet they can change things for themselves and for others, as they allow themselves to alter their states of consciousness within that meditation that they do time and time and again, and become masters of consciousness. And so, you all have a great deal of self-consciousness, you see, wondering what others are thinking, but you know you should put that to one side, because to be too involved with what others think of you can be detrimental to your own progress, and so we would ask you to be positive in your approach, to be a little bit hesitant, maybe, in going forward, but to know yourself and to trust in God will take away your nervous energy, and allow you to have this wonderful experience of being able to link with that spirit within and with God the Creator of all life.

Because the truth is that there is no death, only life eternal, and that is the message that you should give out time and time again, so that other people can see that you are walking the walk as well as talking the talk, to use modern phrases. But you have to be happy within yourself, and if you can find that strength within from the spirit, then you can give of yourself unstintingly and help others, and you know, that is what being of service is all about. Not about self, but about becoming selfless and putting things into perspective so that you can be a shining example to other people, to invite them through the doors of a sanctuary such as this, where the power of thought is constantly in use, through the prayers, through the healing and through the welcome that you give to one and all without judgement, because you know that they are all seekers of truth and understanding of the spirit.

And so, we wish you well in all your endeavours and say to you, your thoughts are living energies and you are all linked to those in the spirit realms by the tie of love that binds one and all together. And so, let your thoughts and your thinking not divide you, but keep you in unity one with the other, fighting the cause to tell the truth that there is no death but life eternal, with progress to be made for each individual through eons of time that you would call eternity.

And so, my friends, we wish you well on your spiritual journey within your physical world and say to you, good afternoon and God bless.

GOOD EVENING to you, my friends (*Congregation: Good evening*). It is a pleasure to come and to talk with you, and to give you and to share with you a few ideas, so that you can go away thinking about the power of the spirit. Because that was the reading that was chosen this evening, to talk about power, because, you know, there are many that are afraid of the power that is within them which is the spirit, and it is proper and right that you should be thinking along the lines that you need to look at the spirit within and the power that it has for you, the individual. Because you all have gifts that have been bestowed upon you, from that spirit that is going to give you eternal life.

For it is that spirit that will make its transition from the material world into that of the spiritual realms. And that is, as you know from your principles, the fact that the soul is what is going to move you, that is the real you, and will take you to the spirit world, whatever your belief system is.

There have been many Masters that have come to the earth vibration to show you, by their actions and their life, how difficult it is to live a spiritual life within the confines of the physical world. And so it may be regarded as a challenge, to say the least, and that is why you have within your Spiritualism your seven principles that begin with the Fatherhood of God, God the Creator of all life. God is a presence that you feel when you look within yourselves for strength, for guidance, for harmony, for peace, for love. Because all of those things are attributes of the Godhead.

Too many in your world of matter seek to have

power over others. And that is maybe the wrong thing to do, because you are all thinking and intelligent individuals that sometimes use power in the wrong way. That causes you a bit of difficulty, as well as us in the spirit world. For all of you have guides and helpers and loved ones that are willing you along your pathway in life, that want you to become spiritually aware. That want you to do your very best for yourself and others, so that you may follow that light that comes from the spirit realms. The light of love that ties you altogether in the bonds of friendship, in the bonds of love.

So it should not be dismissed, this power of the spirit around and about you, as well as within. You have to take, of course, responsibility for yourself and for your life and live it to the full, in the best way possible, for you. And in so doing, others will see how in control of your life you are, and they would ask you questions as to how you remain calm and how you have great trust in God and in the spirit that you are.

And so, if you can but think about God, the Creator of all life, and look into your own gifts that you have, then you are going to walk your spiritual pathway as you should do so, whilst that spirit is encased within the confines of the physical body. It is not an easy task for any one of you. But, nevertheless, you are all moving forward as you should. Because the truth is, of course, that there is no death, that the spirit will make its transition from the physical world to the world of the spirit. And that is the beginning, the middle and both ends of the story.

But too many people stray off their spiritual pathway and only concentrate on the material aspects of life, and this causes a little bit of disharmony within and around that individual, and that is why it is so important to recognise that strength within you, the spirit itself, the true self that you are. And you cannot fool the spirit world and you cannot fool yourself, but you can, indeed, try to fool others by misusing the power of the spirit.

And so, we would just ask you to be a little more considerate to that spirit within and to the spirit world and to God the divine spirit. Because you have all taken your time this evening to come to this place to sing your praises and worship God, the Father, and so it is, because you are all part of the Brotherhood of man. You all know that principle also that calls upon the fact that you will be compensated and retributed for all your actions, for all your deeds in this world, and so, you see, you have to be mindful of your agenda in your life.

So, all that we ask is that you be kind to one another. That you unite together in the knowledge of the power of the spirit. That you may go back through history and times gone by to see the many Masters that have walked the earth, displaying the virtues of the spiritual gifts and the spirituality within themselves. A few choose to look within and to develop your gifts, then you will truly find that power to sustain you through all of life's ups and downs, to give you courage, to give you fortitude, but more importantly to bring to you harmony and peace. And so we leave with you the love of the Father, the power of the spirit, for you to develop as you will, for you to use as you will. But, remember that you must always walk in the light, in the light of the truth that you cannot die, for many people do not ever get over the grief of losing a loved one because they remain in the darkness and in the fear. Because they do not wish to expand the mind, and to investigate and to look within for the answers to the questions that they have. That is why we ask that you to fly the banner for Spiritualism, because it is important for the world, as a whole, and for you, as individuals.

So, we will leave you with this address, to make you think, to make you sit up and take notice and say to you, my friends, goodnight and God bless.

Chapter Four
Cardiff First SNU Church, Park Grove, Cardiff

SUNDAY 16TH SEPTEMBER 2012

GOOD EVENING to you, my friends, it is a pleasure to come and to talk with you, and to endeavour to inspire you to work with that spirit that is within you. For you all have gifts that will unfold to enable you to cope with life in particular, and in general with your day to day living. For there is much in your world that upsets you as an individual. There is much in your world that will excite you as individuals. But there is time within your life, however busy you may be, to look at the spiritual aspects of life. All of you take notice of nature, do you not? Because whether you like it or not, your seasons change. You are now going in to the autumn time, although you may think that during summer you have had winter, because rain has not stopped falling on your ground, and even that has upset the growing of the crops, and goodness knows what else suffered as a result of the unusual climatic conditions, and so you can see the cause and effect of nature.

Over eons of time, mankind have tried to understand the elements but still they throw up questions, they throw things up that means that there is a disturbance within your day to day world. And so that is why we chose the subject of nature, because you are all au fait with the seasons, and as you enter, in this hemisphere, autumn, the other hemisphere, they are going back through to spring and into summer, and so you can say the seasons are reversed where you are in the physical world. But the world keeps turning, as they say, and there are many that are wishing to explore everything and anything to try and answer the questions that they have.

You have seen many, in the past months, show you how with dedication they have got gold medals and been the best in their sport. It has inspired many to take up sport in one fashion or another. But not all will excel to the same standard. But it is in trying that that individual is going to manage to achieve many things in their life. Because when you look at your spiritual development, you have to show dedication, you have to show determination, you have to go with the flow. You have to use your gifts to get the best out of life. You have to also train yourself you see. Because it is in the training that those athletes have worked their way to the top.

Our channel here was listening to the radio before setting foot through the doors, and they were doing a profile on Andy Murray. And when he was first on the tennis circuit and met up with Rafael Nadal, he gained inspiration from that individual, but came home to explain to his family that Rafa trained four and a half hours per day and he, Andy Murray, trained at that time four and a half hours a week. So, of course, he realised that he had to put a little bit more effort into his natural

33

ability to play tennis if he wanted to take on that mantle of being the top of the profession. And so, his life changed at the age of fifteen, when he decided that he ought to leave this country for a tennis academy abroad. And look what has happened, although it has been some ten years before he's finally reached his wish and won the US Open Tennis tournament, in the men's singles final. So that did not happen overnight, as you can see, from that quick resumé, and so it is with your spiritual awareness and development. You have to decide what you are going to put into it and how much time you can spare for it. But, you know, the key is to be of service. We don't expect you to be able to play tennis and serve at, I don't know, in excess of a hundred miles an hour, like Andy would do to win. But we do expect that you give of yourself and be of service to others, and in doing that your spirit is growing and you are understanding its promptings within you. Because that feeling of exhilaration that you have helped somebody else is second to none. No ulterior motive just that you wish to help.

And as it was said in the reading, first of all, you have to help yourself, you have to understand yourself. Why do you want to do this? Why do you want to do that? There are many people that seemed to be called to their profession. Whether that is to teach, whether that is to be a clergyman or woman within an organised religion, they wish to help, and that is what service is all about. That is what spirit is all about. That is what Spiritualism is all about.

Within your religion, within your science, within your philosophy of Spiritualism you have just to take on board the principles that are there for you to follow, for you to think about and interpret in your own way. For you will not fall short if you understand about God as the Father. About mankind as being a brotherhood, because you are all equal. You talk about the ministry of angels, and that is because you know there are those in the spirit world that devote their time to walking with you, each individual that you are. They walk the pathway to inspire you, to uplift you, to help you. And all that is asked of you is that you help others along your pathway in life. There are too many that are only interested in the material aspect of life.

And you know, it is very difficult if you are going to consider the differences between materialism and Spiritualism. Because you will be swayed one way or the other. But to take the middle path is what is asked, so that you do things with the right intentions, so that you understand that death is nothing at all, just the gateway to a new life. And even if you do not understand that and do not wish to consider it, you know it is going to happen, whether you understand it or not.

There are too many in your world that are in fear of the world unseen, or of the world unknown, because it cannot be seen with the physical eyes. And so people turn off their feelings and the promptings of their own spirit just because they are a little fearful. And so we wish to take that fear away and to help you to look at the light that is within you. To look at the light that is around you. Because you can see how the elements change from season to season, then you should be able to accept the change within you when you move on to the spirit realm. There is nothing to fear, for life continues.

And in your principles, they talk about Personal Responsibility, so it is up to you; nobody can convince you of this truth, of life that continues, but we are willing to bring to you all the help that we can. So that all that we ask is that you open your mind to all things being possible. That you bring positivity into your life. That you give of yourself. In that giving, so you receive more and more from that spirit within you that links with the spirit around you and about you.

And so, it is simple really, you know; you do not have to put time limits to what you want to accomplish, for we talk about eternity, for there is no beginning and no end and a circle demonstrates this because, you know, it is just evolution that you are following. Modern day Spiritualism may have been around for quite some time, and there have been other religions that have gone through eons of time, but it does not matter what you believe, as long as you look for the truth. As long as that truth inspires you to move forward. As long as that truth sustains you in times of uncertainty, in times of worry, in times of trauma, because life is for living, you see. And so, we ask you that you embrace all that you can see. That you embrace all that you cannot see. Because it is beyond the confines of matter.

We would encourage you wholeheartedly to use the gifts that you have been given by God, the life force, the Creator of all things. And so, we say to you my friends, look for the signs within nature. Be determined to do what you must to fulfil your own life. Do not be too quick to take on the burdens of others, and that is why personal responsibility is important. You can help but you cannot carry everyone along with you. Decisions have to be made and you have to be kind to others but not forgetting to be kind to yourself. That is all that we have to say for now.

To give you food for thought, because very soon you will be coming into harvest time and celebrating the safe gathering in of the food that is going to be utilised to feed the world. With spiritual understanding, that is exactly what we do, we feed the world, for there are many that are hungry for spiritual understanding and knowledge. It is there, my friends, for the taking, be brave, be dedicated, be determined and train your mind and your body to accept that you are spirit here and now.

It is a truth, it is not a fallacy, and so we wish you well, my friends, on your journeys through life. Long will it continue, for it will continue without breaking. It will just be a transition from one realm to the next. Look forward to the challenges. Take up the cause, tell people that there is no death. Tell people to enjoy life. Give thanks to God for all the gifts bestowed upon you. Not only your spiritual gifts but the gifts that come through nature itself, for food and water and sustenance of the body, and we will provide in abundance sustenance for the spirit. The spirit, that is you, the individual. You are not walking through life alone. For those spirit guides and helpers are always close at hand, albeit unseen.

And so, we say to you, good night and God bless.

GOOD EVENING to you, my friends, it is a pleasure to come and to talk with you, and to bring to you inspiration from the world of spirit, for, you know, you have just been through your Christmas time and now you are into a new calendar year, and you want to do your very best and probably made what you term resolutions to make yourself go forward in life.

And so it is that we would indeed push you forward on your spiritual pathway of enlightenment, because within you is this power of the spirit. And you are in charge of you. You have what you term personal responsibility, and we can only come forward and advise and drop thoughts into your mind from time to time for you to take notice of, and sometimes for you to act upon, because you do not travel your earthly world, and that life that is yours, on your own. There are far too many of you in your world that suffer from loneliness, because you wish, sometimes, to hibernate and take one step away from being actively involved in life.

And so it is that you have to be able to organise yourselves and be positive in your thinking. Because, you know, sometimes you can talk yourself into being negative, your mind racing forward from time to time with the many difficulties and problems that you have to face. That, my friends, is life within the material world. Your media manages, all of the time, to bring to you world events that can cause you great distress. For the world can be seen through the eyes of the camera lens and brought directly to you, through varying media in your advancing, technological world, that seems to be going forward in leaps and bounds. And priorities seem to change every second of the day.

And so, you need to stay focussed on your life and how you live. For if you can find within you peace, then that is what you will exude to others. You will carry it forward in your aura. People will be influenced by how you act and react in your day to day living. It is important, you see, that we help the individual soul that you are to look within for that power, for that strength. To look within for that understanding of the truths of life and the spirit. The spirit that you are now, the spirit that you will be when the physical body is of no more use to your soul's evolution.

And so, we want you to understand that you are all part of that Great Spirit that you call God. That that power and strength within you is for you to use and utilise to help both yourselves and others. And in so doing, you will find peace and harmony. It is very difficult sometimes, not to be carried away when your mind is going forward, in overdrive, trying to deal with day to day issues. And that is why time spent, such as this, within a controlled environment, you can link with yourself, in the relative stillness and quiet and within the energy and power that is built up within this building, through the activities that are held within and through those that come through the doors with their own energy, with their own understanding of the spirit and themselves. The doors must always be kept open to serve the community, to help those that are in need and those that are in fear of the unknown. The truth of the matter is that your individual spirit will transcend from the physical world into that of the spiritual realms of life. That your life will continue.

You have within your Spiritualism seven principles, and they talk about the Continuous Existence of the human soul; that is you, my friends. You have a continuous existence and that in itself is worth passing on to others. For many fear that transformation of the spirit, and you know that at the death of the physical body it is but the beginning of a new life. A different state of awareness and existence.

And so, we want you to take out this truth. We want you to be happy and calm within yourselves so that you can, indeed, understand that you are in control. That you need answers to questions, and you have the right to ask the spirit world to assist you, to help you in your understanding. They say that life within the physical world is one of lessons to be learnt, and indeed, it is so. But in your learning, you are expanding your mind, you are dealing with your spirituality.

You are able, therefore, to help others along your pathway in life. Albeit a smile to uplift someone that may not have spoken to anyone for quite some time, a helping hand, a listening ear; all these attributes that you have you just have to put into action, and so we don't want you just sitting in the power of the spirit and meditating all of the time, because we also need some time for action. Putting your ideas to good use, acting on what you know is right, for you all have your own motives for why you are doing this that or the other.

And when you open your mind and your heart to the power of your own spirit and to the power of the spirit world, then you are, indeed, ready for action. We want you to be harmonious one with the other, as your first hymn spoke about friendship. And it is true that you have to come together on an even playing field, so that you can work for the very best that you can do. To give that power, you will receive that power, in the same measure, so that you will grow from strength to strength. It is important that you do not look back too often, for that is in the past. We want you to look forward into the future; as we said, a new year has just begun, and in that beginning we wish you well with all your endeavours. So remember to look to that Great Spirit that you call God the Father, to enlist all of those that are the brotherhood of mankind in the same actions, to work in the light of the spirit, that is the true person that you are.

We would say to one and all, indeed, venture forth into the new calendar year and keep marching forward, and then at the end of your calendar year just glimpse back and see how far forward you have come, because you may feel that you are standing still from time to time. That is why, at this time, we would say to you, indeed, look forward. The future is bright, spiritual understanding is on the move. Too many look back to the avatars that were; look forward and know those that are working with the light of the spirit, and follow those truths that you know are important. It may seem as though we are asking you to change tactics, but we ask that you go with the power of the spirit as the age of spirituality continues to come to the fore in many minds of many that walk in the physical body in your world. Take heart, take heed, stay positive and know that you are a powerful being in your own right. Use that power wisely, my friends, link with the God force and walk in God's light.

And so, we say to you, good evening and God bless.

GOOD EVENING to you, my friends, it is a pleasure to come and to talk with you,

And indeed, to throw some light on the subject of the Divine Plan, because in your world, you become enmeshed and immersed in materialism, because you are on the earth plane to live a material life, most of which can be enjoyable, but sometimes, you know, you have hurdles put in your pathway that you have to deal with, and many try to skirt around many things, and others try to take things head on, shall we say, and sort things out for the better. For the betterment of everybody involved. And you know, it may be in your world that you are bombarded by the media in various forms with doom and gloom. And yet, you know, sometimes there are heroic works that are done by many in the human race that are never reported on. And so in your world of war and turmoil and strife, there is much good that comes out of the adversity, and it is all what you may say man-made, because there are too many in your world that want power over others and over many things, many lands, many peoples, and that is not right, because you are all spirit and you are all able to have expression of your spirit.

The flowers here in the centre are there in commemoration of Robert and, it was said, for all the good works that he did, because each one of us is capable of good works. And that is because you are working with that spirit that is the very inner being that you are. You may walk through life dealing with, shall we say, smoke and mirrors, giving off the impression that you are this, that or the other, and not allowing your spirit to be your guide. To be your intuitive self is quite a difficult thing, because you all think of your intuition as letting you down, as something that is feeble and frail, but let me tell to you now that it is the physical body only that becomes feeble and frail. Because that is what will return to the earth, and your spirit will transcend this earthly plane and move on into the spiritual realms of life.

And so that should help you become a little more positive in your day to day thinking, whatever is there in front of you. There are many that strive to better themselves through the education system, and there are many young ones at this time of the year that are sort of nail biting shall we say, waiting on examination results, and there is so much pressure put upon them that think that their life will not be as it should if they should not come up to the required standard and pass with flying colours. Because that is what your world is all about, academia, and yet there are many that can change your world just through actions and working with their individuality and their spiritual selves. Because all of you have gifts of the spirit that you are, and all that we ask is that you use them. You know, when there is a revolution in the spiritual sense in your earthly world, then things will change. Not as it did for Saul on the road to Damascus, when he was literally blinded by the light of the spirit, but you know, it will be a change that will be gradual, and as indeed, it was said, long lasting. And that is what we want, you know. We want your world to transform itself, and when everybody realises that if you should happen to kill another human being or animal, then that spirit has not been finished off. The

43

body may be no more, but the spirit has transcended into the realms of light and spirit.

And so, there is no ending as many believe. You see, there is much debate, in these days, on whether there should be help to those that are reaching the end of their earthly road in life. But you know, that spirit will transcend to the realms of spirit when it is ready to go, because that is the law. The law of nature the law of God. Even your kingdom of nature, your natural world, there is death and new life because all the earth goes through cycles that you know as winter, spring, summer and autumn. And so does the soul that you are; your mind and your spirit become the soul that will move forward and then understand a little more about eternal life. And so it is that there are many in your world that are in ignorance and fear of the unknown, of that world beyond that of matter. And so they have difficulty in dealing with grief, in dealing with the loss, the physical loss of their loved ones and friends, or when you see in your media when many seem to lose their physical lives all at the same time, because there is much tragedy within your world, and it will always be so because that is the law, the law of cause and effect.

Within Spiritualism there are just seven principles that are brought to your attention, so that you may have your own interpretation of what they mean to you. For Spiritualism is not a creed or a dogma; you have a mind that thinks well, that asks questions, that wants and requires answers to those life lessons that you learn as you go forward in earthly time, as your soul evolves and want to go back to the source, the source of God the giver of all life. And so, you talk about the principle of the Fatherhood of God and indeed the Brotherhood of Man, for, you know, all humankind are equal in the fact that they have spirit deep within their very being. And you know, also, that there is the principle of the ministry of angels and the communication between the two worlds, so every human soul can communicate with the spirit; it is just that you have bad press because there are too many that are out just to link with the spirit world to have a glimpse of the future.

And yes, glimpses of the future are helpful, but you know, you have to live your own life, you have to be master of your own ship, of yourself that is, and that is why Personal Responsibility is so important as the fifth principle. Do you know it is too important for you to skirt over, because there are laws within the spiritual realm of life, the law of cause of effect, and so that means as you sow so you will reap, whether in this life or the next it is unimportant to you. And so, the motives by which you do this that or the other are the guidance that you need. The guidelines for allowing the spirit to have its own expression. There are many in our world of light that wish to communicate with you to say they are alive and well. But there are only a few that are willing listen, or indeed investigate, to learn about the other dimension in life.

There are many dimensions in life, all told; many search to see if there are alien beings alive and well, and most of you enjoy a good sci-fi, although it can cause fear to rise up in an individual. Within Spiritualism we like to put fear aside, we like to bring to you the love, the harmony and the peace and the encouragement for you to embrace all of life, whether that be in the spiritual realm or in the physical realm. We urge you to look for answers to your perplexing questions, most of which are laid at your door as soon as you switch on any form of communication with your media.

And so, we want you to search, we want you to understand, we want you to know that if you understood that your spirit will be forever, and you will be forever, in some form of existence, then you would not grieve for a long, long time. You will always have to go through a grieving process, of course, because you are grieving for the loss of the physical of your loved one or friend. And life changes, you see, when one moves on to the spirit world; there is a gap in your friendship circle or in your family circle and one has to come to terms with that loss; everybody in that circle has to do the same.

And so it is that we want you to embrace the world of the spirit, that we want you to look and understand the Divine Plan so that you can feel full of hope, full of life, full of love, for yourself and one another, for it is in service to each other that the spirit has expression.

And going back to the horrors of your world, there are many that work only wanting to help others in their suffering, and there is much that comes through in medical science and innovation from those war torn countries, but you know what we want most of all is for everybody to live in peace with each other and one another. But you can rest assured that the Divine Plan is progressing as it should, but we want more and more people on board so that you are not suffocated by the doom and gloom, that you do realise that there are many heroes and heroines in your world.

Not so long ago they were commemorating the event of the First World War, and I expect many of you wondered what have we learnt in those hundred years? Because still there is war within your lands. Maybe there always will be until the Divine Plan settles in your world of matter. But we tell you all, be brave, have faith, have trust, use that love within you. Not the love that is celebrated in February every year, but a deep love just for the humanity that you are part of and belong to. We in the spirit world will strive always to bring forward the truths of the spirit that there is no death, that death is but continuance of life.

And so, we say to you, my friends, good night and God bless.

GOOD EVENING to you, my friends, it is a pleasure to come and to talk with you.

And to bring to your attention that we in the spirit world do encourage you not to be engrossed in fear and despair. But, you know, in your life you are always confronted by what you call death. When you lose loved ones and friends from the physical realm, then you are entitled, indeed, to grieve the loss of their physical presence. But you know, that is only the beginning for them of a new journey in life.

And over recent weeks you have been subjected through your media to all the atrocities in your world where people seem to think that they can just bombard others out of the physical world, and that is instilling fear into others, to use a modern phrase, big time. And, you know, there are many that would tell to you that it is this reason, or that reason, and many of course blame religion and fanaticism that goes into the mix. But, you know, it brings with it that fear that is instilled in your very being, if you are not aware of that very fact that life continues and life cannot be taken away, only the physical can be taken away from the physical world. It is important, therefore, that we bring to you peace, that we bring to you understanding, that we bring to you love. For those are those things that you need to hold on to so that you can remain strong, so that you do not become enmeshed within fear.

Death cannot sever was what Silver Birch was talking about, and he also spoke of fear, that mankind seems to carry with them day to day. Because, you see, as you are sensitive to your own spirit and to the spirit world, then you are going to be sensitive to what your media produce. They do not produce answers to questions. They just bring up more questions for you to find answers to. And, you know, they always seem to blame religion, they always seem to put the blame on God the Creator. Because they do not want to take on any personal responsibility, for news is never uplifting, it is always depressing and discouraging. It is never, ever something that you feel good within yourselves when you have finished listening or viewing or researching on your Internet. There are so many factions that all seem to have answers for you. And it is up to you to take control of what it is you are doing in your life, because if you show love to another then you are going to be shown love in return. If you show hate to another then you will receive hate in return. It is the law of cause and effect, you know.

And it is mentioned, is it not, within the seven principles of Spiritualism itself, in that principle of compensation and retribution for all the good and evil deeds done on earth? If the media have their way, they would bombard you with all these evil deeds that appear to be going on, and that there is no answer, and so that causes more fear within the individual. In fact, there is one country, now, that is what you would call in 'lock down' because of fear of those that are termed terrorists. It is all words and labels that are of no use in the greater scheme of things. You see, you may all wish to wear labels, but when your spirit, your soul, returns to our world it is known by the colour that you carry, the light that you are. You do not wear a label saying that you were a Spiritualist, saying that you are of any other religion. It does not matter.

You know, don't you, when there are children born into your family or to your friends, the surge of love that is experienced on welcoming that child into the world; well, that is how it is when your spirit returns to our world; there is love there waiting to be shared with others, and then you can see the mission that you were fulfilling in your physical life. There is no hatred or acrimony within our world, for you will realise that you have done well in the work that you have undertaken. It is not all about the difficulties in life, it is all about how you handled the difficulties in that life. How you helped yourselves and how you helped others: that is what the power of the spirit is all about. To be of service, one to the other.

The media have not covered the heroics of many that allowed the power of the spirit to surge within them, to help others that were all in fear of what was going on, when those terrorists were causing mayhem in various parts of a country, or indeed of the world. Many helped those to move on and out of danger. There were those that worked tirelessly to aid those with injuries when they were able to get to the hospital. Everybody put their best foot forward, so to speak, and that, my friends, is the power of the spirit in action. For the physical body is nothing much; shall we say that it is just a vehicle to be used so that you can have a life within the physical world. The essence of you continues. Life continues and the physical world is left behind. Difficult, indeed, for those that mourn the loss of the physical presence of their loved ones, but it is good for you to know that that life continues.

And then, you see, light will come to those that grieve and mourn. They will understand through their own spirit that there is, indeed, communication between the two worlds, the Communion of Spirits and the Ministry of Angels. How many have sent thoughts out to all those that have made their transition in such unfortunate and unusual circumstances. Then, of course, there are prayers for those that caused that fear, that caused that violence, that caused that trauma; they too have been in the thoughts of many. For they, perhaps, have not understood that they cannot reign over others through the power of terror. The power of love will prevail, but it may take eons of time before the human race can, indeed, display that love from within, for then peace will reign in your world of matter.

And so, you see, we don't want you to be devastated, to be afraid, to be upset. We want you to understand the truth, that the spirit of each individual is alive and well, it is just that their physical life has been terminated. Not finished, though, just terminated as being a physical being. And you call it a human being, but sometimes you wonder where the human is, because some people do not act as though they are indeed part of the human race, for they are radicalised; they are in fear because their minds have been overcome with what others are telling them is the truth. That is why it is important that you go out and tell your message that death cannot sever loved ones from your being. It is important, also, that you talk about the principles within Spiritualism, for there is, indeed, the Fatherhood of God, and in that principle about the Brotherhood of man, there is no separation; and yet within your human world you

51

separate, and you should be coming together. There should be no separation. There should be no difference between humankind, for they are all of that same essence, that of the spirit.

So, that is the message that we bring to you, so that you may, indeed, dispel fear, that you may, indeed, bring hope into your mind, bring peace into your being, and demonstrate to others how you understand life so that they may be touched by their spirit and understand that there is more to life than that of the physical world and their own physical selves. Then, you see, you will feel empowered to face life day to day. You will feel at peace with yourself, you will feel that love that comes from God the Creator, that you can share with each other.

And so it is that that power that comes from God the Creator, the Father, is beyond labels of religion. For it is all the same essence and it keeps your world moving forward, although as we say, too many want to bring fear into the equation, and we want to bring peace. Allow the peace bringer to dwell within you, and you are going to move forward in your understanding, and that will allow you to influence others in your service that you give, one to another. As we said, no media coverage of the heroic acts, when people were helping each other to move out of the trauma that they were facing unexpectedly; they all came together to try to aid each other. Let us do that, in our day to day living: aid each other, for in that aid it is, indeed, spirit in action, and so we leave with you, my friends, the peace and the love that comes direct to you from the Fatherhood of God.

Good night and God bless.

GOOD EVENING to you, my friends, it is a pleasure to come and to speak with you.

And we would also say to you welcome to that great understanding of the fact that you cannot die, and yet in your world that is all that you seem to be bombarded with, because you sit, day by day, hour by hour, in your media, whatever form that takes in your modern world of technology. And so it is that you would think that we could get our message across a little bit better, but as you can see, not many open their minds to the understanding of the world of spirit and the fact that your spirit survives physical death, and that your loved ones are closer to you than you can possibly understand when you are locked into your physical mind and your physical body and your physical world.

And so it is that soon, you know, many will be telling to you from the science point of view that there may be something beyond the physical human being that you are. Because, you know, God the Creator has given you this spiritual aspect of yourself. The real you, the person that you truly are. Everyone has come to the earth to live in duality of the physical and the spiritual.

But as that reading said, the material, physical world takes precedence for many, many people. And yet you have heard so much about the life of one young lady that was an MP that was out on her own mission to help as many people as she possibly could, and in so doing to live a life also where she had a partnership with her husband, her family and her children, and the grief has been shown to the world, from the point of view of that family. And yes, it is a great tragedy, of course, we are not belittling that, but the great truth is that her spirit is free of the bonds of the physical body and the bonds of the physical world, and she can continue her journey in life where she will be aspiring to help as many as possible, including her own family. She will not leave their side as she tries to inspire them, to uplift them through this period that has to be gone through that you call grief. That is part of life, my friends, and difficult it is, because you do miss the physical presence, and time is a great healer, they say, but you still have to get yourself from A to B through that difficult time. And so, we need to, to uphold each other in times of crisis, in times of adversity, in times of grief.

So it is important that you understand this great truth. There are many principles you know, well, seven, if you are counting, within Spiritualism, and today, in your physical world, you celebrate Father's Day, and so you honour the father that you may have had, and perhaps did not have, but you all have that father that is God the Creator, and you know, life can be difficult if you do not have the presence of a father figure in your life, because the father you know is symbolic of somebody that helps you along life's journey, from babyhood through childhood, adolescence and even through adult life. And so, it is good to give thanks, you know, to the human form of your father and indeed your mother on that relevant day also in your calendar. And so it is that parents, whether you are close to them or not, do play an important part in your life, and the lack of a parent certainly has its drawbacks on the individual who may be a baby, a child or an adult. There is never a right time, you know, for you to lose contact with a parent. There is never a right time to lose contact with a child or any other loved one, when the physical is lost back to the earth and is no more within your material world.

And you know, sometimes, when we are struggling to understand life, it makes us look further, further afield from that of the physical. And that is why whatever religion you follow, it does not matter, for the Creator's presence is what you are looking to understand. A presence that you may not be able to see, in the physical form, and yet the beauty abounds within the world of nature and within the animal kingdom also. For, you know, they live on their instincts, animals, and they look after one another and they learn survival techniques also, so that they can live together, albeit that they're very different species that have different roles to play in different parts of your earth environment.

And so, you see, we can go on and on and on, but we can assure you that all the thoughts and the prayers that you send out to your loved ones are held in high esteem within the physical world, and the communication between both go on. You may all think that you have a vivid imagination when suddenly you are thinking of that loved one that you lost recently, or indeed some time ago, because they follow you and your own progress and they help you to understand life. They give you strength and courage from that inner spirit that you have, each one of you, in abundance.

And you know, in adversity, that is when you rely on that spiritual essence of self. And yet when you are in a period of everything's going along fine, you do not understand that that power and strength is still there

55

with you, that you can share with others. For it is indeed true that your actions are more important than your thoughts. Sometimes, you know, you can hurt another with the spoken word, but we try, when we come forward to speak, to enlighten you with the spoken word. We do not wish to put fear or misunderstanding into your mind, for you are all able to think rationally and carefully. You know, not many have mentioned the man who was the perpetrator of the crime of the loss of life of Jo Cox. But he, too, needs help and thoughts to go out to him, for he needs to understand that he is more than the mixed-up mind of his mental state at the moment.

And so, the spirit world are aware too of his needs, and you know it is important that we send out thoughts for all those that are less fortunate than ourselves. The power of thought, the power of prayer works beyond your wildest imaginings, you know, and so you have to spend a little time in reflection of what you are doing and why you are doing what it is you are doing. We encourage you all to walk in the light of that great creator that you call God. For you cannot go wrong, you can only grow in stature and understanding, but the more questions that you have answered, the more questions there will be, as your knowledge base is thirsty for more knowledge and understanding and so you will move forward.

The reading spoke of the many different aspects of the spirit realm from that of the astral plane that replicates your world, so that nobody, whatever their understanding was, can be left without moving forward, and they then want to ask questions, want to expand their spirituality and their understanding, and so move slowly forward with the help of those that are on the higher levels that can descend to the astral plane to advise, to show the way, so that they have a greater understanding of the truth. So be brave, my friends, and go forward, through that time of coming to terms with your grief and your loss, but in so doing you can help others who also, at some time or another, will go through grief and loss. Through your experience you are qualified to help others in their loss and in their misunderstanding of the fact that you are not dead when you have died, you are alive and well.

And so, my friends, we leave you with these thoughts, so that you can go forward showing the banner of truth, showing your true colours, shall we say, of your understanding of life and of continued life, beyond that of the physical realm. That is what is important. You cannot tell somebody else what to believe, but you can explain your beliefs. You can show the strength and courage to the world, to the individuals that are willing to listen. You cannot persuade anyone, but you can show them by your own actions, your own deeds, how strong you can become in the face of adversity, when life is lost, for age is no barrier to moving from one state of existence to the other.

And so, my friends, we wish you well on your continued journey in life. Hold that banner high, and indeed, you are able to climb many mountains when you look for that spiritual strength within you, the individual. And then in supporting others you gain in strength, you gain in stature, you gain in many ways that will allow your spirituality to unfold whilst you walk the earthly path in life. Be brave, be courageous, use that power wisely and take your personal responsibility on your own shoulders.

We say to you, my friends, good night and God bless.

Chapter Five
Newport SNU Church,
Charles Street, Newport

SUNDAY 27TH MAY 2012

GOOD EVENING to you, my friends, it is a pleasure to come and to talk with you.

And to give you a little bit of inspiration, because, you know, you are all capable of very many things. And you all have thoughts, do you not? You all have to, at one time or another, keep your thoughts in check. Because it is not always wise, is it, to say your first thought to somebody, in case you say the wrong thing. And so, you are always thinking what is right and what is not so good, and you keep up your own level of right and wrong.

You all have a moral code that you follow, and surprisingly, you know, you learn many things from the influences of other people around and about you. Because, you know, the best way is to lead by example, because then your actions are speaking louder than words. And when you are happy with what you are doing, then other people are influenced by your mood also. How many of you have been somewhere and immediately have sensed an atmosphere that things are not quite as they should be, because somebody has had a disagreement and you happen to walk into the room after it has finished, but it has disturbed the atmosphere. And so, all of you, you see, to one degree or another are sensitive to those around you and to the atmosphere that is around you, and if we were to line you all up in the middle of this church one behind the other, very close together, you would all soon be moving because you would want a little more space around you, because, you see, as you become enclosed in say a queue, then your auric field is going to want room to move, and that makes you feel restless and discontent. And so it is that you need to take notice of what your inner being is telling you, because that gives you signposts along the way as to the right or the wrong path to follow, and your spirit is wanting expression. And so, you all have to take on board personal responsibility, and it is up to you what opportunities you take and what road you take in your life, because you have to be content with your choices. Nobody is going to tell you that you have to follow this path or that path or the other path, because, as you decide on certain decisions, then you know whether you have to do a U turn or not because of how you feel within yourself.

So, we bring to you encouragement, you see, so that you have a little more confidence within yourselves, because there is more to life than you can see through your physical eyes. There is this spirit within that gives you the whole concept that you are something that is going to have a life of eternity to live. You are not going to die, you are going to change your habitat, shall we say, you are going to go from the physical realms to the spiritual realms at that point that you call death.

As difficult as that may sound, transition is as easy as it is taking an inbreath for the oxygen that you need to sustain your physical body, to sustain your physical life. It is nothing at all. It is just a moving on, and so it is that to have that understanding will allow you to be open minded and open hearted to all things being possible, to know that the love tie that binds you in this world continues in the world beyond matter in the spiritual realm. And so, there is no difference of that love that is felt one for the other, but the big difference, of course, is the fact that the physical body is no longer with you. And so it is that you have to grieve the loss of the physical body of your loved one. That is part and parcel of coming to terms with the transition. It is always easy to talk the talk, to use a modern phrase, but it is not quite so easy to walk to the walk, to be able to tell to others how your own belief in the spirit within and the spirit world that interpenetrates your world, but you know, by the way that you are and the way that you act, other people will take notice. They will realise that it is worth listening to what you have to say when you put it over in a down to earth manner.

There are too many people, you know, that want to say things just for the sake of saying the words. But when you say it from your heart, there is meaning behind it, and through experience you will be able to help others who are facing the loss of their loved ones and are grieving. There are many in your world that only look at the darkness and the sadness that they have encountered through life, and that is why we want to bring people through the doors of this church and others like it, where they talk always about the afterlife. About the life that is to come, that you prepare for day to day in your day to day living, and in the way that you think. You are, they say, as you eat. They are also saying that you are as you think. And so you are responsible for your thoughts, and you know, at the end of the day, that to be kind and to help another that you see is struggling in one way or another in life, then that is giving of yourself, and that is being of service to your own spirit and to the spirit world.

So, at every turn in life you are tested. Not that you have to pass or fail that test, you just have to learn from it and move on and then realise that you are indeed a strong individual that can cope with all things, because the spirit within is strong and the spirit world are there walking beside you every step of the way.

It is important, you know, that you understand that you are not being stalked from the spirit world by your loved ones and your guides and helpers, because sometimes they have to stand back a little bit. Just as you would if you were a parent to a child, you wouldn't be able to be constantly with them, because you have to allow your child a little bit of breathing space, do you not? You cannot attend school and be with them twenty four seven, but you can listen to what has happened in their day, and you can be part and parcel of their lives by just helping and telling them that you understand, and so it is with those that link with you from the spirit world; they are forever listening to your thoughts, because, you know, you do not have to say things out loud, and the spirit world uses your mind to communicate, and so your thoughts are very important to you and to them also. Because, you know, you cannot think one thing and not be honest with yourself and honest with the spirit world. They know what you are thinking, they know what you are doing, and so you just have to keep yourself in a positive mind, knowing that the spirit world will not ever let you down.

You have as a first principle within Spiritualism, talking about the Fatherhood of God. Because God is the essence and the Creator of all life, so you cannot journey on your life's pathway in the physical world alone. You are accompanied every step of the way. You may be prompted at times to do things that you think are a little bit rash, because you know they need you to be responsive to the spirit world. It is important that you do check your thoughts, that you do have time on your own, that you are able to feel the presence of those that would come into your auric field, to tell you that they still love you, to tell you that they are there and to tell you that it is easy to make that transition. And therefore, you should have no fear of the future. Things are good, things are bright, when you look at it with your spiritual eyes. If you only look at things through the material, physical eyes, then things do indeed look a little dismal, a little dark and a little upsetting, and so we have to extend our vision to that of the spiritual aspect of life. And if you can quieten your mind, and if you can accept that your loved ones have made their transition, then you will be halfway to understanding yourself and being able to move forward in your life. There is no need to feel despairing, to feel discouraged; we only ask that you feel that it is not as difficult as you think. Accept that you are being given strength, that you are being given courage, and your thoughts will indeed change as you go forward in your life, as you begin to understand the truth that there is no death, only life eternal. Just remember that because life is continuous, you are forever progressing.

If you can take time out to have time to think and meditate and gather your thoughts, you will gather strength also. So do not be afraid to sit in the silence, because within yourself you have these ideas, these things that inspire you to lead you forward in your life, and so we ask that you be positive. That you are guided and strengthened from that spirit that is you, the real person that you are. Because you know, sometimes, when you sit and you think, you do wonder, well, Who am I? What am I? Where am I going? What am I doing? Take the bull by the horns and look at the spirit that is you, and things will begin to fall into place. You may have a little difficulty at first, sitting in silence, or listening to music, but you know you cannot be afraid of yourself, you have to have within yourself confidence, and you will then become aware of all these others things, because they will be added unto you. And so we just say to you, my friends, walk on, walk tall, and you will be surprised at how you can take on board all the tragedies of life that will come to you from time to time, because your life is only for a short time within the physical environment.

And so we would say to you, my friends, good night and God bless.

GOOD EVENING to you, my friends, it is a pleasure to come and to talk with you.

And perhaps to talk about the world unseen, and perhaps to talk about getting the message of Spiritualism across to the younger generation, in particular, because, you know, it is important that these young people are taught about the spirit within themselves. Because there are many talented ones within that younger generation, and yet they do not fit in, maybe, to the education system that is not, what shall we say, moving forward. It is a little draconian in its attitude, and school days are not what they were. And yet it seems with changing rules and regulations that respect seems to have disappeared. Not only within the school environment but within society generally. And you know, these youngsters have great enthusiasm, and they do need to know the basics of education, just as you all need to understand the basics of life, especially within the material world.

And so it is that there is this world that you call unseen, those that have passed through the veil of death, those have moved on into the spiritual essence of themselves and of life. And so that spiritual world, that spiritual realm is, as you may describe, intangible. But nevertheless, it exists, and so that is the main message within your Spiritualism: the spirit continues. There is a continuous existence, and that is what everybody needs to understand, whatever level of education they have attained within their material world.

And so, you have many that may be described as genius, you have many that are described as not being very good within the mental capacity and within the learning capacity, but within the spiritual capacity then there is always room for progress towards the light, towards that power that you call God, and it is a progression. A steady progression. And so, you see, you have to understand that there is more to life than what can be seen with the physical eyes.

There are many in your world that are grief stricken at the loss of their loved ones and friends, because age is no factor in when that spirit will leave the physical body and move on in life. And though it is difficult to face up to the parting of the physical, of your loved one, it is something that happens day in, day out, and it always will. Because life cannot be sustained within the physical forever. But life can be sustained forever when you take on board the spiritual aspect that is there to explore, that is there to understand, and that is why we want to kick start you into your understanding of yourself and your own spirit. And it is, my friends, the lessons of life in the material world that allows your spirit to expand, because you are always asking questions and seeking answers that are within you. But you look for them beyond yourself. It is very important, therefore, that you look to that essence and that strength within yourself, because it is a great teacher, and so you can learn day to day.

You are always in control of your life, although at times it may seem to you that you lose control of your life. If you have learnt to drive a vehicle, then you know that, whilst you are sitting behind the steering wheel, that you are in total control of that vehicle. That you can make it go fast or slow, that you can turn right or left, that you can drive backwards or forwards. You have been taught to do so and have had to show to others your competency before you are allowed to do it alone. And so it is with that analogy in mind that you are preparing yourself, due to the lessons you are learning, to be in control of you, the individual, and so when you pass to the spirit world, you will the see the results of your actions. You will evaluate your own life. You will not be facing your maker, so to speak, and be told the errors of your ways. You will see what you have accomplished by the way that you have acted, by the way that you have thought, by the way that you have taken on responsibility for yourself and, from time to time, responsibility for others.

Because you are all teachers; you help others by listening to them, you help others by advising them, but nevertheless people do not always take notice. And experience is definitely a good teacher, and if you have learnt your lessons well, then you do not go back over things that you found difficult, because you have learnt the way forward. And so it is with those that have reached their new life in the spiritual realms. They are still interested in those that they link with through the tie of love.

And it is important that they see that you are doing right, that you know right from wrong, and so it is important that you are able to lead by example and show the younger generation how to open their minds to this great power of God. How to live a spiritual life. You know, it is important that you learn right from wrong as you grow up throughout your childhood and into adulthood, that there are markers along the way to keep law and order in your land. Just as there are markers in the spiritual world also, so that you keep on the straight and narrow, because, you see, there is a principle that talks about compensation and retribution for all the good and evil deeds done on earth.

You have choice, my friends, in how you react; you have your own set of morals, you have that guide within you, and so we would urge you to take notice of your feelings, of your intuition, because this is your guide into what is right for you and what is not so right for you. It is also important that you understand that, although progress may be difficult and may be slow, it is attainable to one and all. To those in your education system that perhaps are unable to grasp the basics of your language, of your arithmetic, of many other things, they can still go on to lead a fulfilled life, but may need extra support if they cannot read or if they cannot write their name, but it does not mean that they are without the understanding of the spirit within themselves. They may be able to demonstrate the gifts of the spirit far more eagerly than those tied up in formal education, striking through whether something is right or wrong. You all have a working, thinking mind; you all have varying abilities.

And so, you may, yes, despair about the younger generation, but there is much talent, and you know, they do wonder about the world unseen. They do try and explore, and some may even use substances that you may think they are abusing, but those substances can open their mind to the realms of light beyond that of matter.

And so it is that if you are taught how to sit in the

silence, that will indeed open your thinking to the realms of the spirit. You do not need substances to enhance that. I'm sure that there are many of you that would know when you have had a bit too much to drink; your inhibitions disappear, and you are more open to the influences of those people around in the physical and to those people around you in the spiritual sense. And so it is that you grow in understanding of that spirit within, of the real person that you are.

So do not despair about the education of the younger ones, because we in the spirit world can enhance their enthusiasm, because they want to live in a better place than they feel that they are now. They want things to improve in the material world, and many are hiding their light from the world, but it will glow and it will grow, and just as an example of that, you can see many that have worked in science and come along with many good ideas in medical terms that have helped many to live a longer life within the physical body. And so, you know, you cause the years within that physical body to extend year after year, and yet there are those in your world that do not get the same opportunities, and they happen to pass into the higher life at a younger age, due to war, due to famine, due to all the atrocities within your world, because there are many of humankind that stay in the dark. They do not become enlightened by their own spirit. And there are many Masters that walked the earth showing the illumination of the light that they were, and many followed, and yet, you know, knowing and understanding about the spirit and the fact of its continued existence from one state to another has not brought to your world peace and tranquillity, as you would expect. And that's because many are looking for power over one and all. And that cannot be allowed.

And so it is that your world will continue to evolve until, in many years hence, people will become enlightened and your world will change as a result. The masses, young and old, will be educated, educated of the spirituality that is within. Educated that there is a world unseen, educated that all your actions have consequences, and then you will begin to see that your world will become a harmonious and peaceful place. So, think always of the world unseen, as you go about your day to day living. Help those that you can by being kind and considerate and respectful, and then you will begin to feel better within yourself. Forget all the trauma within your world and link in to looking at your own traumas in life, and trying to understand why this is happening and why that is not. Ask questions of the spirit world, and you will become enlightened, slowly but surely, until the time comes that you, as an individual, will make your transition to the higher life, to those realms of light.

Put your faith into the younger generation, and you will soon see things turning around, or shall we say turning about, because, you know, when you have the wind in your sails, you have to turn the craft about so that you are going in the right direction; that is what needs to happen, my friends, in your world. So remember, the world unseen is there, vibrant, and those in the spirit world are asking that you take on board your own beliefs and help others in finding that understanding that there is no death.

We tell to you all the time the same message: that

there is no death. My friends, believe it, know it, understand it, and use that great knowledge within you to educate those young ones about the truth and reality of life. And then you will see how the masses can become affected by the positivity that you have, by the knowledge that you have. Spread it far and wide, and you will soon see that, although Spiritualism seems to have lost its way in enticing those young ones into its midst, The spirit has not lost its way; it is vibrant, especially within that young person. And so it is that they have control of life, but we have control of spirit, whether the spirit is within the physical or within our world. Progression goes on, marching forward, so progress is being made, but you may not be able to see it, you see all the bad within the youth of today, but we would ask that you look for the good within the youth of today, for there is much that is being done.

There are many that serve in countries far and wide and give of themselves, of their knowledge, of their understanding within just the medical sense, and they are doing good work in helping those that are oppressed by those that are wanting power over others. So you can rest assured that slowly by surely spirit has the upper hand, that the young generation and those that are to come are being educated by those in the spirit world and the understanding of their own spirit. So give thanks for that world unseen, send out your thoughts and prayers so that things may change within your world for the better.

Always look on the positive aspects of life, and always be thankful for the gifts bestowed upon you by God the Father. For it is in God's power that things will evolve as they should, and so remember that that is the truth about life. You may not be understanding of all things that are educational, but you always understanding of your own spiritual journey in life, when you begin to question 'What is life?' 'What am I?' 'What are you?' We are all channels for the spirit, so use your gifts wisely and have great faith in that younger generation that are out to change the world for the better.

And we say to you, my friends, good night and God bless.

GOOD EVENING to you, my friends, it is a pleasure to come and to talk with you.

And we do in the spirit world thank you all for your thoughts of remembrance on this day when you as individuals, and as a nation, remember all those that lost their lives in the many wars that have occurred throughout eons of time.

We would also like to say to you that we would endeavour to bring into your work positivity, in order to create peace so that your wars may diminish in time. For in your modern world there is always dissatisfaction, there are always those that want power over others, and the only way that they know to keep that power is keeping those in the masses oppressed, and so you have what you term warring factions.

But your world is one of many lessons, and so it is that you are going to see various things that will upset you, that will unnerve you, that will frighten you, that will cause you distress, and there will be those that will lay down their lives, their physical lives, in order to bring about peace. Because, you know, you have to fight for what you believe in, but that does not mean that you have to kill and have enemies. The power of the spirit within mankind can change things for the better. But it is when the head rules the heart that you have problems within yourself and within your world.

It is important, therefore, that you understand some of the truths within your religion of Spiritualism. Within your religion, whatever that may be, because all religions talk about God as being the Creator of all life, being the deity that is to be worshipped, to be understood, for that power is of good, and there are those that would use that power that comes from God to bring about destruction within your world and that is not what should be occurring.

It is important that you look within yourselves for understanding of life, because your life certainly does not end at that point that you call death. It said in the poem, did it not, that the spirit moved on, and maybe you do not have the physical presence of your loved ones with you day to day, for there will be an empty seat, an empty chair at the table or within the home, of where once a loved one sat and was companionable to you. But, you know, that personality, that essence of spirit, has only moved forward in life. It is only the physical body that is no more. The personality and the spirit, which you may term the soul, lives on in our world of light, in our world of understanding, in our world of love.

And that is why we want to bring to you positivity. Because in remembering all those that have passed under the conditions of war, it can be a little bit demoralising for the future. Because in all the days that have gone by, and in the remembering of those souls that have lost their physical lives, it does not seem to have had any good effect upon the lessening of war in your world. For there are uprisings in many countries, and there are those in very poor countries that suffer because of man's inhumanity to man. And so, mankind has to come to terms with their actions, and with their deeds and even with their thoughts, because, you know, we want you to find peace within yourselves. And in so doing that peace will move out into the ether and join with the peace and the love of the spiritual realm of life. And then there will be transformation within your world of matter.

And so it does matter to us what you are thinking, what you are doing with your life. Every one of you should take notice of the promptings of your own spirit too many of you dismiss, spirit communication, by saying that your imagination is running away with you. But you know, you all have a connection with the spiritual realm. You all want to understand life a little bit better. Because if your life just ended and the spirit did not return to the spiritual realm, then your life would not make sense.

And so it is that we are mindful of your principles within Spiritualism. And as people fight against religion, and people become fanatical in their beliefs and then seem to want to terrorise others you will understand that you are, that is, mankind, a brotherhood. All of equal measure. That of the spirit. So why fight each other? It is not good. It is harmful to your earth vibration. It can be harmful to the spiritual vibration also. If you are going to continue to be enmeshed within materialism itself, it is not long before you will be celebrating the Christmas time, which is significant in regards the birth of an avatar that came to show people the way, through the light of the spirit. And so you should be mindful of that spirit within you, because when you become a channel for the spirit world, then you can bless those that come into contact with you, using your gifts of your spirit to bring healing, to bring upliftment, to bring positivity, to bring harmony, and so it is that we bring those positive aspects before you: to give you food for thought, to feed your spirit, as you would daily feed your body. There is nothing that we can say that will stop mankind fighting for power, but we can assure you that your world will continue, and even through the rigours of war there is much that comes forward from those that would wish to serve and be of assistance to those that suffer. Many go out as doctors and nurses that bring in provisions and food, so that many are saved to continue to live in their environment that they know. And so all is not lost, and so we bring in the positive aspect of when the spirit within you is moving you forward to be of help and assistance to another.

So, everybody as a spiritual being has work to do. And even those that go into religious orders do not come out into the world as you know it. They too help, because they dedicate their lives to always be prayerful, and to ask for help for intervention from God the Great Creator to bring that peace into your world. And so, everyone will have a part to play, so remember those that have passed before you, friends or family, for each one has a life that will continue, and so be mindful that there is no death. The spirit and the soul of the individual is there with you, watching over you, helping you, giving you assistance.

All you have to do is be honest with yourself and look out for that great peace and calmness that comes to you when you least expect it, for that is truly your spirit leading you forward into the light, into the light of peace and tranquillity. And so we leave you with the peace from the world of spirit, so that you may feel calm, that you may feel assured, for there is nothing to fear in life, there is nothing to fear at that point that you call death, for you will all go through that veil of death and return to the world of light.

So be positive, do not be anxious, as your world continues to fight. It is important that you always look to the light and walk in the light of God's grace and love.

We say to you, my friends, good evening and God bless.

GOOD EVENING to you, my friends, it is a pleasure to come and to talk with you.

And to perhaps answer the many questions that you have, from time to time, that bother you, because your world always seems to show you turmoil and strife, and then you worry about the world. Many years ago, you would not see what was happening further afield than within your home environment, but you have news and media and goodness knows what in this technological age. And so, it is that you have a great awareness of what is happening within your world; indeed, maybe a greater awareness of what is happening in the universe, for there are many that explore space and want to understand that solar system and want to understand how matter was created. Where is, and what is, the big black hole?

And then there are those that open their minds to the spiritual aspect of themselves, and this is where we come to the fore, because we want to encourage you to think. We want to encourage you to work with your spiritual selves, with the essence that you are. We want you to become channels for the spirit that you are. For those that will walk with you in your life, unseen, maybe for most of the time, but nevertheless there to assist, to help and to guide. Because, you know, you do not walk the earth and your earthly life alone. You may sometimes wish to look over your shoulder because you feel a presence from the spiritual realm. But you think it is your mind and your imagination playing tricks with you, but you know, it is very important that you understand about your spiritual selves and your spirituality.

Throughout eons of time many Masters have walked the earth; to show the light of their spirit has been their mission. And there have been many things that have been documented to many of the Masters, and you know they all link with that spirit within and with the world of spirit outside of yourselves, and have produced that essence of being true to oneself, and to the understanding of God being the Father. And whatever nation you belong to, the essence within mankind is the same, that of the spirit.

And so, in that regard, in God's understanding you are all equal. Whatever belief system you have or indeed do not have will not hinder your progress from the material world to the spiritual realms, because it will always be a natural transition, and then you can see beyond the confines of matter. And that is why we ask of you all this evening to think about your spiritual work. To think about your motives, to think about how you treat yourself and others. Because that is what you need to work upon to bring that spirituality out into the open. To speak of your knowledge and understanding, of your own self. To help others that may be facing crises that you have been through yourself, so through that experience you can just tell your own story, to help another that you see to be in distress.

Over the last few days, weeks, months, you have seen stormy weather lashing your physical world and your environment. And you can see the natural power that is behind the sea, behind the elements of nature and everything in that world of nature, seems to be what you may consider a little topsy turvy. And you can see how small your existence on the planet is in the greater scheme of things. When there are disasters that they call natural, then mankind seems to blame the essence of God. But you know, within the world of spirit we do not bring our wrath to bring you to submission of understanding the power of the Great Creator that you call God. For those in the spirit world come to aid and to assist, and that is why we want you to take on board that you can live a spiritual life, and in so doing you become kind to yourself and so kind to others. And you will be of service to God the Creator. You will want to find peace within yourself, and as you do, so peace will transcend into your world within the physical existence of life. It may sound a pipe dream, but you know, as long as you dedicate yourself to looking at life through the eyes of your own spirit, then things will look much better than they do when you cannot see beyond the confines of matter.

There are many in your world that fear the transition of death. But it is as has already been said, a natural occurrence. You have to move on, because your physical body only houses the spirit for a short time, so that you have learnt a few lessons along the way, that you have enjoyed a physical life. As harrowing as a physical life may be, with its ups and its downs, you should endeavour at all times to see the good within yourself and within others. Because that is looking through the eyes of the spirit. Read your books, read about the lives of the Masters to get some inspiration as to how you should put one foot forward in front of another, to move yourself forward in your understanding. Because, you see, you may have many questions and you have to find answers, because what you are doing is searching, because you all have your own ideas, you all have a mind of your own. And sometimes, inadvertently, you put up the shutters so that we, in the spirit world, can't always get through as clear as we may wish. You are always thinking that your mind is tricking you, where, in fact, you are being helped along the way. You are given strength, you are given courage, you are given many things that will transcend you into that greater understanding that love conquers all.

Again, that may sound a cliché in itself, but it is always the love tie that binds you together with those that you consider that you have lost to the spirit world. All that you have lost, in essence, while you are here in the physical, is that physical presence of your loved one, of your friend. And so it is that we would encourage you to look at the seven principles for example, because they are open to your own interpretation, and we have already mentioned quite a few of them in this talk so far. We've mentioned the Fatherhood of God, the Brotherhood of Man, Personal Responsibility and the Continuous Existence of the Human Soul. We would remind you of the Communion of Spirits and the Ministry of Angels, because it is those in the spirit world that keep you going; whether you feel their presence or not, it is irrelevant, but if you allow yourself to understand that they still do exist, then it will bring to you joy and comfort and peace. And then we talk about the fact that there is retribution and compensation for all the deeds done on earth, whether they are good or bad. And that means that nothing will hinder your

81

progress, because it doesn't matter, but you will have to make amends, you will have to look and see the opportunities you may have missed to be of assistance to others.

And so, when you look at all those things, you may think that you have a steep mountain to climb, but all that we ask is that you put one foot forward at a time, and as long you have the right motivation and you are trying to help yourself and in so doing giving help to others by your very actions, then the good news is that you cannot fail. And so, that is why we ask of you to dedicate yourself to understanding your spirit, to understanding yourself. And that will move you forward, albeit slowly in some cases, and maybe too quickly in others for you to grasp exactly what it is you are doing and where exactly you are going. The only way is to move forward in your understanding of life.

So, we give you a little insight into what you have to do as an individual, to open your mind and your heart to that great power that you call God, so that you may be, to some extent, blinded by the light of the great love of God the Father. And when you come to that realisation, you can walk forward. You can tell the good news to those that are struggling in their life, for there are many that never really move forward from the grief and bereavement of their loved ones, their friends, their children, whatever relative they happen to have lost.

And as you enter a new year in your world, you expect things to improve and you look forward with positivity, for you know that things have to work themselves out, and there will always be ups and downs in life. But we can assure you that with the understanding of the spirit and truth that there is no death, then you are strong within yourselves to be able to confront whatever obstacle is in front of you, and that you will pass with flying colours all those trials and tribulations, and you will be able to be of service to the Great God, the Great Spirit that is love eternal.

And so we leave you with the blessings from the spirit world and give you that courage, that strength and that energy to move things on, so that you feel at one with yourself and those in the spirit world. And so you can find then peace, you can experience love, you also experience that harmony that you need so that you can, indeed, be about God's work. For the world that you live in, my friends, needs that light and you to work for the best possible outcome that is on offer when you are faced with adversity. When you do understand that you cannot fail, you can only move forward, then you are indeed beginning to understand that your spirit is the real person that you are.

So, remember that it takes dedication, and when you are feeling a little low, remember that we have asked that you dedicate yourself to the spiritual things that are important for you and for others. We bring to your world, always, light, for it is in that light then the darkness is dispelled. Too many people fear the unknown and yet the unknown is just the continuance of life itself.

And so, we say to you, my friends, good night and God bless.

SUNDAY 13TH APRIL 2014

GOOD EVENING to you, my friends, it is a pleasure to come and to talk with you.

And what shall we say to you, this evening? Because, you know, just looking at your world at this time, then there is much to cause you disillusionment, we shall say. And yet on a day like today, when the sun is out and everything is starting to blossom forth, in this time that you call spring, then it does renew your hope, you see, because it is important that you do not dwell in despair, because there are so many things that in your world, indeed, cause you despair and disillusionment, because things seem to be precarious so many things happening within your world, within different countries and so, then, you begin to worry about being safe.

And too many in your world despair when they have lost loved ones and friends to the spirit world. So we cannot reiterate enough the fact that the spirit within mankind will move on in life to a life beyond the confines of matter, to a life that is lived in the spiritual realms of existence. And so, your loved one or friend is not lost or gone, because they still have a life, albeit a different one from that of you that is still in that material existence. And as you move forward to next weekend, when the religious festival of Easter is celebrated, then that too reminds you of a beginning of a new cycle, as spring emerges out of wintertime. And so it is that whatever winter has brought into your world, it has not stopped the new cycle beginning with the springtime.

And so it is that that brings you hope, hope in the future. Because, you see, it is a matter of concern for most of you that the physical body will not give you life for an eternity, because it will only have a certain time to have an existence within your physical world. The body, to many, can be more than troublesome, because of health issues that befall one and all of you at some time or another. That is why we must tell to you that this form of existence, within the material world, is indeed short lived, but we have to tell you, as we do all of the time, that the spirit within you will move forward and just transform itself into our world and fit in very nicely.

And so, you see that should take away fear, for many fear, as to what the future may hold. But we want to give you more than hope. We want to tell you that your spirit will definitely move on throughout different life spans, you see. It is important that you understand your own spiritual self, and in so doing you will find peace. You will find hope; you will find strength and purpose. For you see, you do have lessons to learn from your material existence, that is true also. And you know, you don't always understand the purpose of this life's existence, or this incarnation of your spirit into the physical body that confines it. But it is up to you to work with it and listen to the promptings of your own spirit that links you, or should we say anchors you, to the spiritual realms of existence.

How many of you here dismiss some of the communication that you receive directly from the spirit world? You tell yourself that you have an overactive imagination, or that this, that and the other series of events are just coincidence. But we tell to you that it is all in the greater scheme of life. And you do indeed have communication with the world beyond matter. I know that many of you may think about the great universe that the earth exists in, and even that immensity of it, can blow your mind. So we do not intend to blow your mind when we talk of your own spirit and the spiritual existence forever and ever, but we just wish you to have an open mind and to open up your heart to the promptings of the spirit, so that you can be of service to those from the spirit world that would walk with you.

Because, you know, it's all about how you can help others in their time of need. Because that is what existence is all about; it's not about just yourself. And in doing service to the spirit, then you do indeed find renewal of hope, so that you do not feel so much in despair or alone, because when you lose a partner, then you do feel that loss significantly, but it does not mean that it is the end of that individual's life.

Of course, it is the end of that individual's physical life, physical form that you knew and loved. And so it is in the sharing of love with one another that you learn from each other, and so you are encouraged to tell what you understand of your Spiritualism to others, because that also takes courage, because people do not wish, some of the time, to know what it is you have to say, and they think that you are a little bit, what shall we say, bonkers is a good word to use. Because you see, it sounds as though it is too good to be true, what you are saying that there is no death, but true it is. Because there is death but only of the physical form. And so, you see, it may be a play on words, but it is also encouraging to think outside of the box, as they say in your modern-day terminology.

You all have communication these days with the

telephone that you can carry with you; before your telephone conversations were confined within a building, within your home, or office, but never when you were out walking on the street. But we can tell to you that communication between the spirit world is not confined within any building, it is there twenty four seven. And just because you have these mobile devices with which to communicate, it does not mean that you are any better at communication, you see! And you know, people will perhaps send a text rather than speak to someone face to face. And so it is in our world also; we do like to have mediums that we can use as a means of communication between the two worlds; we can do it directly to you, yes, but sometimes you need to be in convivial surroundings, you know, so that you can talk to each other and share your experiences, and in so doing give direction to others by the way that you live, by the way that you cope with grief and other traumas of life.

Unfortunately, you see, you have to learn day by day, and so we bring to you hope. It is important that you never lose hope, because that is positive, you see. Keeping your mind alert to all things being possible keeps you, my friends, on the straight and narrow. Looking outwards, looking upwards, going forwards and not living in the past. By all means use your memories of your loved ones to keep you going, because those memories cannot be obliterated, and when you make that journey to the spiritual realms of life you will meet up with all those near and dear to you.

I can hear some of you thinking that there are one or two that you would rather not see again. Well, we tell to you that that does not matter; you will meet who you wish to meet and who wish to meet you. Those that you have loved, those that you have held dear in your hearts, those are the ones that will come forward, and even those that you may have had difficulties with will be there waving a white flag and offering you comfort at making that transition from one world to the next.

And so all of that, you see, should keep you uplifted, should keep you balanced, should keep you in that state of being able to have your communication when and wherever you wish. Because, you see, we can transcend the confines of matter, and so it is that we are always able to assist. Maybe not in the physical way that you may need assistance, but we can definitely stand beside you and give you support and, more importantly, share our love with you, so that you do not feel alone or without aid.

Most of your charities, in your world, are always looking for aid, for assistance in the monetary form, more often than not, but you know just to give of your time to someone else is what you would term being very charitable; it is not about money or financial help, it is about investing in people. You are people who know people, and so you have this big responsibility to invest wisely your time, your effort, and then you will begin to feel much better within yourself, must more at ease and much calmer in your mind; and that is what we are wishing, for every one of you is an individual and from time to time need a boost to remember what is important.

We go back to your Easter time and tell to you of the rebirth of life in your world, but we have just spoken to you of rebirth in our world; when the physical body is no longer of assistance to your soul, then your spirit will transcend and transform that energy that is you. The real person that you are.

So, take from this what you will, but remember to always be hopeful and positive and you cannot fail to work and move on in that spiritual light of God's love, the Creator of one and all. So, as vast as your universe may seem, please concentrate on yourselves and give yourselves that encouragement. Remember that hope is so important. Never lose sight of it. That will keep you positive, and when you are welcomed home by all your loved ones, into our world, you will see what a good and faithful servant you have been to the spirit that you are.

And so, we say to you, my friends, good night and God bless.

(Address based on the acronym SBNR – Spiritual But Not Religious)

GOOD EVENING to you, my friends, it is a pleasure to come and to talk with you.

And to perhaps shed a little bit of light on that acronym for you. Because, you know, many of you are afraid to stand up and be counted. And you know, your Spiritualism is a recognised religion and therefore followers of Spiritualism could call themselves religious. Because it is defined as a religion because, you see, you talk about the Fatherhood of God, you talk about the Brotherhood of Man, and so it is that you understand that you are spirit here and now, and it is the spirit that gives you eternal life. And so that means that death can be banished from your vocabulary.

But, you know, there are many in your world that are distraught when they are grieving and feel bereft at the loss of their loved ones to the spirit realms of light. But do you know, it does not matter what religion you should follow, what label you should wear, what belief system you have, as long as you utilise the gifts of the spirit that is the real you. And so, therefore, if your quest is to be of service to God, and you understand the spirit within you, then you are going to unfold your very own spirituality. And, therefore, that is what is important in life, in your world of matter. Because the world of matter, you see, is what confines your spirit, for it is encased within the physical body, and the physical body only has a certain time span, and so we would encourage all of you to perhaps label yourself SNBR.

And so it is, you see, that you are not wanting to be

pinned down by the confines of religious beliefs that have been in your world for an eternity also. Because there has to be structure, you see, in your world, and eons of time ago structure was maintained by bringing fear to the people, to the masses, for fear meant that they would conform. And yet their spirituality managed to shine through even the great person that you call Jesus; a medium in his day, his spirituality shone through the adversity and the pressures of the world in which he lived, the Roman Empire, wanting control, wanting to control the masses.

And so, he turned within himself and to the spirit world to bring forth all the spirituality that was his, and to encourage it within his friends and his associates. And that has borne forth, through time, the religion of Christianity. But you know when things are written and things are told by word of mouth, then some of the authenticity of it all seems to dissipate and disappear, and that is why we want to encourage you to work on yourselves, to find peace within yourselves, and peace will then come within your world, through your endeavours in your own day to day living.

And so then you can tell that you are indeed spiritual without the confines of dogma or creed, as long as you are doing what you are doing for the right reasons and with the right motives, and that you think the best of yourself and others, and you want to help those that you think are less fortunate than yourself. Then you are truly on the road of expanding your own mind, your own understanding, you are asking questions of the spirit world, of God the Father, you understand that you are indeed all spirit, whatever religious belief you may have.

It does not hinder you in giving of yourself and being spiritual in your understanding and in your thinking. And so, therefore, it is acceptable for you to be spiritual but not religious.

And so it is that you can link with many in your world of varying religious beliefs, and stand your ground and still use your own spirituality to aid you and to aid others. And so it is simple, you see, that we ask of you to be spiritual rather than religious, so that you can break the confines of all the rules and regulations bestowed upon you by the varying religious beliefs. You can see in your world how some are compromised and become fanatics, as you might say, and are weaving their way through the world trying to be martyrs to extreme religious fanaticism and causing trouble and strife, and anything but acting in a spiritual manner. And so, we have to tell to you that the spirit within will conquer all, for the spirit world guides you day to day, for each one of you has guides and helpers that draw close to you. And it is your conscience that you should be taking notice of, for when you feel uncomfortable within yourself, then you are doing the wrong thing. When you feel that you are doing right, and being fair, then you are doing the right thing and so you are very much guided by your own mind, by your own spirit, by the soul that you are. For it is the soul that will transcend what you call death, that situation when you have to make a journey from one state of existence to another.

And so, indeed, it is good that we have you here, because you are spiritual but not religious. Then you have an open mind, you have an open heart, and when you give of yourself then that is when you feel that you are doing God's work, that you are, indeed, mounting the obstacles of life. For there will always be obstacles in your life, my friends, for it is a school room of learning, the material realm of existence, but in that learning, the spirit within you becomes stronger and stronger, and when that work and that learning is done, that is when the spirit will transcend from the physical body, back into the realms of the spirit world. And that is what you term transition. And then you will see that there is compensation and retribution for all the good and not so good deeds done on earth. You will see the bigger picture, my friends, and that is good. And you will see that you have worked well, and so we will welcome you back to those light workers, shall we say, that touch your earth to provide continuity between the two states of existence, and so it is that you will understand more about the communication of spirits and the ministry of angels. You will understand how close that world is to yours and that you are guided in times of adversity and trouble, so that the strength within you keeps you up and running.

Communication in your world, these days, seems to happen through mobile data, shall we say, with either text or calls or goodness knows what, and still you have your arguments and you mistrust one another, because communication is not any better although you have better means, shall we put it that way. You will see that communication through the power of thought from our world to yours is something that is spectacular, shall we say. And so, when your spirit is not confined by the physical world, then you will understand all things. And so, you have an eternity with which to progress your soul towards that figurehead that you call God the Father. And so, it is your personal responsibility to take charge of your spirituality to shine that light forward, and that is why we would say to you, do not be confined by the belief systems of worldly religions.

Take on the broadest sense of structure that you have within the seven principles that you can interpret as best that you can, and it will lead forward, slowly but surely on the spiritual pathway of life that will run parallel with your physical pathway in life, your material pathway in life, and then when the two run together, at the same speed, you will feel content within yourself. You will be looking for joy in your life, you will be thinking harmony and love, and God's greatest gift to all is love. It is not confined to your world of matter. It joins the two worlds together, and so it is that we will allow you to be spiritual but not religious; it should perhaps be the new emblem for Spiritualism, because it would draw a lot of people through your doors because many do not want to be confined with dogma and creed. And so, you have a legacy, my friends, because you have an ability, all of you, to link with the spirit world, because you all are spirit. And that gives you this powerful means of communication that many people are afraid to look at, to investigate, to use. So we would ask you to use your mental ability, we would ask you to use your psychic ability, we would ask you to use your spiritual ability, and then you will indeed be powerful within yourself, and things will start to change within your world.

Do not take too much notice of your media, because turmoil seems to be everywhere in your world, with mankind still striving to control the masses. So, be up for the challenge, be spiritual, and then you will see that your life will begin to change for the better. You will feel fulfilled as a person, you will be able to help others that are perhaps not as open minded as you may be or so open-hearted as you may be, and so it is that we encourage spirituality.

So, look to that light and focus on the love of God the Father, and you cannot fail to accomplish much, as you begin to understand who and what you are, here and now, in the physical realms of life. So, be not afraid of that word death, for it is but a continuance of your life; that is, I think, what is important. So, indeed, use that acronym if you will, if it will make you more happy in your life. If it will make you more encouraging of yourself, if it will make you more tolerant of others, then you are, my friends, winning the battle of spirituality in progress.

And we say to you, my friends, good night and God bless.

GOOD EVENING to you, my friends, it is a pleasure to come and to talk with you.

And to say to those that are, what shall we say, familiar with my voice, with my words, we thank you for your, what shall we say, continued support in those words that we bring forward. Because you do not seem to tire of what we have to say from the spirit world, and that is good, because that means that we are feeding your soul. We are feeding that psyche that is your mind, and the spirit that makes up your soul, and so it is that we welcome, coming to an environment such as this, so that we may inspire others to look at their own individual spiritual pathway in life. Your material world is not an easy place in which to reside.

The reading that was given spoke to the Divine Plan of action, to use a modern phrase. Because, you know, your world is in what you may call turmoil. Because everybody is seeking to have power over others, over lands, overseas, over the whole inhabitation of your world. And so it is that we need to bring to you positivity and an understanding of that Divine Plan, because each of you has a role to play in your world of matter. It does not matter what you think you can do, or you cannot do, because of physical restrictions or even maybe mental restrictions on you, the individual. The spirit within can transcend and work through those physical problems that you have, through those material problems that you have, through those emotional problems that you have because that is life in your world of matter. But the spiritual realms do have not the restrictions and the confines of the material, physical world in which, at this moment in time, you reside within.

And so it is that we are always welcoming you into the midst of an environment such as this, where things of the spirit are spoken about, because you all put your promptings of your own spirituality to your overactive imagination. You dismiss the promptings of the spirit. You dismiss when you have communication with the spirit world, in your daydreaming state or in the state of dreaming within your world of sleep, and then you just push those things that are unseen to one side. And some individuals never do act upon their own intuition; they want others to help them to make decisions in life, they want advice from their friends and loved ones. And yet, you know, many do not take advice, even when it is given in the correct manner, between communication, between you and others. And yet, you know, all of you are quite capable of making your own decisions, because you are responsible for you. And within Spiritualism that is in the principles, and has been said as the phrase Personal Responsibility.

And so it is that we in the spirit would indeed, from time to time, come to advise, but you know, sometimes advice is not good enough, for there are many that have to learn through experience, and that is the best way to learn, but perhaps the most uncomfortable way to learn, and that is why we are always looking out to have those that will work with their spiritual understanding and their spiritual gifts, that are bestowed upon each one of you, because it is the spirit within that is necessary to give you eternal life. And so, with that knowledge that you are going to live for an eternity, which is very difficult to comprehend, we would tell to you that all of you have gifts that you can use to help others and, in so doing, to help yourself.

In your lives, you are all worried and concerned about others, about yourselves, about those that have left the world of the physical, because it is necessary that you have this mind that will turn things over, turn things upside down and inside out trying to find answers to questions; and that is what you like to ask questions of those in the spirit world. Test the spirit, they say to you. Through eons of time there have been those that have come forward to show their spiritual light, to show their spiritual understanding, to link with those in the spirit world that have a message to give out. There are too many in your world that grieve over the loss of their loved ones and friends, and yet do not think that it is possible that the spirit has managed to move on when the physical body goes back to the earth.

And so it is that we would encourage all of you. The thing that was said in the reading was that it won't be a blinding flash that will change your world; it will have to be through those that are ready and willing to act as channels, and there is no one on your earth plane that cannot be a channel for the spirit world. It is just there are many that you may think have been brainwashed into matters that make them, how shall we say, terrorise others to get power over your earth vibration. But you see that cannot be, because it is the love vibration that comes directly from God, the Father, that is the vibration on which to work. That means that your motives are most important in the greater scheme of things. If you do good then your spirituality will grow, your understanding of the spiritual realms of life will flourish. You will understand that the material and spiritual pathways in life have to run parallel, one with the other, and then, friends, there will be a transformation within your world. And that is what everybody is waiting for. People will lay down their arms and not pick them up, as they do now because they are on that vibration of greed, they are not on the vibration of love. Not the love that you celebrate, once a year in February, but the unconditional love that lies within you that is part of the spirit that you are.

And so, you see, the spirit has to have expression, and that expression does not begin when the physical body has failed and gone back to the earth. Spiritual expression can start as soon as you are ready to listen. You know, in these war torn countries, you see them fighting on the streets; what you do not see is how the power of spirit works within that environment, helping those that have been injured, helping those that need shelter, food, that need help at the very basics of life itself. That is how the spirit of the world works.

We are always, in our world, helping those to express love to one another, and that shines forth in war torn countries and in those countries that do not have enough food, or water, to sustain physical life also. There have been many things that have come out of those countries, under those dire circumstances, that have helped the world as a whole. Even those countries that have spent very much money in exploring space, all that was not wasteful, as it may seem at first glance, because there have been things that have been understood that now help those in your world that may suffer with the physical body not working as it should.

And so, all things have an upside, shall we put it that way, and that should give you encouragement, that should help you to have faith in yourself and the spiritual realms of life. And so, the Divine Plan is unfolding as it should, but it is just that most of you, in your world, have what, we would term, blinkers on, so that you cannot see too far ahead, that you cannot see the full picture of how the world will, indeed, follow that Divine Plan. You may not be in your physical body, as the plan unfolds, but even so you will be part of the plan, because your spirit is going to continue for an eternity, and then you will see the part you have played in your life, whether it be just your physical life or in the spiritual realms also, because that life will continue.

And so, we want you to go and tell the message about the truths of the spirit, that the spirit cannot die, that the individuals that you knew on the earth are still individualistic in the spirit world, bringing back to you their memories because it is the love tie that binds you all together. And so it is that it is important that you take your rightful place in looking for answers to questions that perplex you in your day to day living. You know, everything changes, and nothing ever stays the same. And yet you all fear change; that word to most is a little bit unsettling, you see. But things are changing, things are improving, because we are able from the spirit world to link with all those that live in the physical world, and when they take notice of their own spirituality, then that is a sure sign that things will change for the better.

And so, we want to tell to you that there is no death, it is only the physical that is left behind, and life continues. So let us rename that event that you call death and call it rebirth, because it is a rebirth into that world that is there steadfast and strong, helping all as they move forward in their lives, giving them an understanding of the fact that the spirit will continue, that life continues, and if people in your world understood just that, then they would look at their lives differently. They would change the way that they do this, that and the other, and that is when true enlightenment will bring forward spirituality, and in so doing the Divine Plan will be unfolding as it should.

And so, we leave you with that positivity, we leave you with that understanding that death is nothing but rebirth.

And so, we say to you, my friends, good night and God bless.

GOOD EVENING to you, my friends, it is a pleasure to come and to talk with you.

And to, indeed, enlighten you about a few truths that are there for you to understand. For each of you has a thinking mind, that, indeed, does become enmeshed within your world of matter, within those powers that be that bring to you the so called news, some of which is devastating, brutal and upsetting, to say the very least. When you come in through doors to a church such as this, then we wish the atmosphere to be peaceful, to be calm, to be encouraging, and to be a place where you can have a short time to allow yourselves to think. To allow yourselves to link with that spirit within you, for it is that spirit that gives a zest for life within the physical world. A life that you should be enjoying, a life that should be uplifting, a life that should be pleasurable to say the very least. But of course, the life within the physical world is one in which you are learning to understand yourself. It is just as you learnt when you were growing up; you learnt to walk and talk and then you were taught things to allow you to function within your world.

And so it is that you all have an ability to do many and differing things. For each one of you is a unique being; you are there for a purpose and you spend life helping yourself and in so doing helping others. You form together partnerships of friendship and more so of partnership as you go through life. For you have to have others to make you feel fulfilled within yourself. Through eons of time the message has been given by those Masters that have walked the earth to tell to you that this is but a road you travel for a very short time in the greater scheme of things. There is more to life than can be seen with the physical eyes. You all have the ability to feel, to understand that you know certain things. It is a knowing when you link with that spirit, for it will guide you forward.

All of you have lost loved ones, friends, to the spirit world, and some of those passings may have been traumatic, may have been difficult to understand. For there is no right time for a spirit to leave the physical body and the material world. For there will always be a sense of loss of the physical being that has been there and touched you in some way or another.

And so it is that when you look and you understand that you, all of you, have an ability to communicate with the world of spirit, then that is a giant step forward for you. Because, you know, when you do get communication, you usually throw it out of your mind and tell yourself that you have an overactive imagination, because you do not understand the promptings of the spirit.

You know, it is important that you communicate one with the other. It is important, indeed, that we in the spirit world communicate with you also. For we cannot live your life for you, but we can assist you, we can give you strength, we can help you in those times that are a little difficult to say the least. But when you look around your world through your media, by various means, then you begin to wonder where, indeed, is God in all this that is trouble and strife. And indeed, all that seems to happen in your world that is shown to you is that of killing, that of war, that of famine, that of illness;

all these things are brought up in front of you so that you cannot fail to notice all this bad news. But, you know, God indeed is the power that gives life in your world and in our universe. For God is the Creator of all things. The earth upon which you live, you are custodians of it. You seem to take, without wanting to give back, and use all these resources to aid the individual. The individual wants power over the earth, but that cannot be allowed.

The power of the spirit will ensure that there is always going to be an earth world, because it is a world in which you live as a physical being whereby you are learning, all of the time, about your spirituality, about the spirit within you, the spirit that will transcend, back from the density of the earth vibrations to the world of spirit. There you will find peace, you will find love, you will find harmony. There is no discordant note in our world. It is in your world that there are many things that you have to endure and come to terms with. But when people, in the name of God, fight and kill each other, then it is not, indeed, anything to do with God the Father, the Creator of the Universe; it is to do with mankind misunderstanding the power of the spirit.

And so, you see, it is all needless, and it is all a bit of a problem for others in your world, because there seems to be no end to the idea that one sect wants to rule overall. Mankind has to be put in their place sooner or later, and it is only going to happen through showing love, one to the other. You have heard that adage, have you not, 'love conquers all'? And so we want you not to be worried about the future of your world, indeed, about the future of your own being, because you know people do not understand that, when they take life away from an individual, that life still continues in our world. And so it is that that life is indeed not snuffed out in any way. Those that do not understand that the spirit moves on in a different dimension, they have to go through the grieving process until they understand that their loved ones are still around and about and understand what they are going through.

And so it is that, you know, in our words, we would say to you your world is almost barbaric, but that is not to worry you, that is only to say to you that nothing will be achieved by man killing man, or indeed by man killing animal. There has to be a respect for each individual, and the fact that they are all part of God the Creator, and so you are all equal, irrespective of what you believe, irrespective of what religion you follow, irrespective of what you think is right or wrong, because your physical mind has been conditioned so that you lose all sense of reason, and that seems to be what is happening with some of these in your world; they want to become martyrs to the cause, do not understand that there is no need to lose physical life to become aware of that world that is beyond matter. God will always ensure that everything happens for a reason, that through the rigours of war and famine, the strife in your world, the power of the spirit interweaves, and there is much that is done to help the individual that is suffering.

And so it is that it is really your media that are giving to you a one-sided version of all the events, because they want to bring to you sensationalism. They want to say to you that things in the world are all not so good. Whereas we in the spirit world want to encourage you to see the light, to see God's light of love, to see that all is not lost. All we ask of you is that you look within yourself and do your very best to send out your thoughts to aid those ambassadors in our world that bring healing.

There are those that through their strength of spirit go out into the world to help and give aid in those countries that are suffering so badly from war. Fights between man will always continue; you have made many peace pacts, and you celebrate the fact that it was a hundred years ago that the Great War occurred, and yet if you look around, war still occurs. And so it is that unless men become enlightened, and we include women also in that term, they have to become, what shall we say, changed by the very idea that the spirit is the real person that you are. The body, the physical body, is but an overcoat that you wear. What you think and what you do is the important issue. No one will be left out from God's great plan; you will all be included.

You are all what you may term a cog in a wheel. You are all precious in God's sight; you are all on the earth for a purpose. You understand the work that you have to do to keep yourself in the understanding that death is but a gateway into new life. Within Spiritualism, you talk about the Fatherhood of God, the power of the Great Spirit; the power of God the Father is what keeps your world ticking over. And the world will exist for a long, long time, just as the spirit world exists for an eternity. The one has to go in line with the other. And so there can be no devastating ending. Things will always change, and the energy that you are, the spirit that you are, will not end, it will only transform. And it is that power within you that we wish you to work with, so that you can use the gifts of the spirit that you have as an individual.

The reading talked about power. And the power, my friends, is within you. Do not look to others to do the work that you have to do. Indeed, look to others for support, for that is good, that like-minded people come together to seek answers to the questions that they have. We in the spirit world enjoy coming forward to bring to you that upliftment that you need, for life can be certainly dull and it can be one of drudgery, especially when you are going through that grieving process of losing your loved ones to the spirit world. So be brave, my friends, and take it on your shoulders to give out this message that there is no death, that life continues come what may.

You know, all this doom and gloom deals with death, but no one ever gives a thought that that individual's life still continues. You know, all those that join up to serve their country and are sent out, not knowing whether they will return in the form of the physical, they have to write letters and be prepared for the time that they may make their transition to the spirit world, and yet day to day you are a little shy, shall we say, to talk about death, to get yourselves ready for something that is going to happen whether you like it or not, but you do not know when that day will come.

We ask that you just bear in mind that that day will come, but it won't be one of oblivion, it will be one of understanding the new life that you are going to have, without any shadow of a doubt. We wish to dispel that doubt, we wish to tell you, time and time again, about God the Father. You are all equal in God's sight, and so within Spiritualism you talk also about the Brotherhood of Man. You see, there are all these divisions depending on where you live, or what the religion within that environment is. All those things set out to divide; we set out to unite you all in that understanding that you cannot fail but to move forward. Whatever life has done to you within the material sense, all the materialism will be left to one side, and you will then be free as an individual spirit to move on and to understand what love is about, what power is about, what contentment is about, what indeed that life beyond matter is all about.

And so, we wish to say to you, my friends, live in that power of God's love that is within you. And we say to you, good night and God bless.

GOOD EVENING to you, my friends, it is a pleasure to come and to talk with you.

It is always good for us to have a voice, maybe a slightly weaker voice than we would normally be able to use, but nevertheless we are coming forward to give you all that upliftment that you require at this time.

You may have been celebrating the Christmas time, and especially the new year, the arrival of which sometimes in itself brings a little bit of fear of the unknown, the future. Because you are all able to see what has occurred in your lives over the past twelve months, but are unable to see what is to come in the next twelve months or so; because, my friends, that is life in your material, physical world. And we wish to banish that fear from you all. Because you must trust in that power of the spirit that is within you.

The power of the spirit, my friends, is what gives you eternal life. It does not matter what your belief system is or what religion you may follow, or have given up in your years of life on the earth. It does not matter. What matters is what you do, is how you think. We don't want you to have closed minds; we want you to use your thoughts as you go from day to day, for it is your mind that has direct communication with the spirit world.

You hear, all too often, of people that suffer with problems of their mind, and yet, you know, it is just sometimes that you become undisciplined in your thinking. Sometimes you are worried about things that you cannot do anything about. For you are all listening to the news, to the media, and the only news that they bring forward to you is that of distressing events in your world. Hardly ever are you given good news by the news channels of the media. Sometimes it is very difficult to find something in a newspaper that is going to uplift you, because it is always a little bit depressing to your mind, your mind of the logical things of life. That is why it is so important that you question the spirit world, that you use your thoughts wisely, because you are able to do many things when you put your mind to it. For the power of the mind can be great upon the body and upon the spiritual being that you are.

And so, you see, you have everything under your own control. For the spirit world cannot live your life for you. That is your personal responsibility. You are in control of you. You have to use your logical, thinking mind just to get up in the morning, or just to go to bed in the evening. Because you are programmed, shall we say, in your world, to live within the physical confines of that world, and of the physical confines of your mind and your body. But your thoughts are free and easy. You can ask as many questions as you would like, and the spirit world will try to find the answers to encourage you to move forward in your life, to face the many obstacles that are there before you, because your world is one of learning, of understanding that there is more to life than that of the physical, material world. The spiritual realm is alive and well, and God is always able to help the individual. The power of God the Creator of the universe is sometimes beyond man's comprehension, for the physical mind is perhaps locked into negative thinking.

And so, we bring to you positivity and understanding that you have much to live for. You have much to do within your world. You have responsibility for yourselves, and many of you take on responsibility for others too. And you give of yourself in service to helping those that you can along your life's pathway. That help may be a listening ear, a helping hand, a smile, a nod, a wink, so that somebody else realises that somebody cares for them, so that their life is lit up too.

You may have heard over the Christmas time about all those that may be lonely, that cannot reach out to others, for they are confined in some way or another; but they are only confined by the physical body and by the physical world in some regard. But their spirit is free and ready to seek answers to many questions. Those in the spirit world are often able to get back their messages of love and encouragement to their loved ones and friends, just through the dream state that you enter every time that you allow your body to rest by way of sleep or maybe meditation. They will take on any challenge that you give to them to wish you well in all your endeavours. For life is not to be endured within the physical, but to be enjoyed within the physical.

Unfortunately, you will always have to meet that problem of losing loved ones and friends from the physical vibration, at that point that you call death, but you know, that is not the end; it is but the beginning of new life for them. But it may seem for those left within the physical world that it is the end, as part of them seems to be lost as their loved ones have left. But slowly but surely mankind can overcome the grief of losing their loved ones, when they open their minds and allow thoughts of their loved ones to enter in. For as soon as you think of them, then they are with you in thought, in that process that we dismiss, most of the time, as having an overactive imagination, or the fact that there may be coincidence and there is no foundation that you may be thinking of their smile, of their laugh, of their chatter, of them being there with you, the individual. Unfortunately, life is about loss. But life is also about living.

And so, we want you to re-dedicate your thoughts so that they become positive as you enter into a new calendar year of 2015. Dispel all the controversies of the times gone by. Remember things with fondness and with love, and that will bring back to you all the positivity that you need to face all the obstacles that you find in your pathway of life. Remember, you are learning all about the power of God the Father. You are learning about your own immortality. You are learning about life that will continue regardless of whether you reside within the physical world or within the spiritual realms of light.

So, we would ask you to remember fondly all those that have made their transition during this Christmas and new year time, when everybody wishes to celebrate, and yet life continues to throw at everyone those things that cause us to feel upset and dismayed and despondent about life in general. This time of the year brings darkness and coldness and bleakness, and yet behind the clouds the sun still shines, but is invisible to you when it is a cloudy, dark, dingy day. The sun, my friends, is there, and so it is with the loved ones that you have lost. They are there too, willing you on into a greater understanding of life eternal.

And so, they are very happy in their new home, that

they perhaps were a little bit hesitant about accepting when they were on the earth plane. But you know, we prepare all those before they make their transition from this world to the next, as you define it, and they are all helped on their journey to make that transition from the realms of existence that are there as part of a natural occurrence. They are all given healing on their arrival, they are all given help so that they may keep the ties of love that bind them together, allowing communication to take place when everyone is feeling that they are able to accept the love of their friends and family.

For when you lose your loved ones to the spirit world, emotions run high, and sometimes when your emotions are raw, then those loved ones stand back to allow you to heal in your mind, and use your thoughts to help you to remember the good times that were had. Everyone makes progress when they return to our world, and so we would wish you well on your progress within your world to tell out the message that there is no death. If everybody took that at face value, then your world would begin to resonate at a much higher vibration and your world would accept that period that you call death as a period of rebirth.

Just as now you will see the nights lightening out and your world springing forward into the next season of life, it is important that you allow yourself to find the peace and the love that is given to you, without any strings attached, from God the Father, the Creator of all life.

And so, we ask of you, to be brave in your new understanding to allow those that you know to grieve the loss of their loved ones, but to give them the

113

understanding that their life continues in another realm of existence, unseen by many, but always there within your thoughts, within your understanding, within your mind.

And so, we give to you courage, we give to you love, we give to you understanding. Please accept these gifts from the spirit world, that are bestowed on each one of you. Do not think that anyone is left out, for you are all deserving of God's love and greater understanding of life. This may be the beginning of a new calendar year. Let it be the beginning of your understanding of your own thoughts. Create in your mind what you wish to achieve, and achieve you will. Because life is all about progression within your own understanding of yourself. In so doing, you will be able to give of yourself to others, to help, just by being you. That is all that the spirit world asks of you.

So, take courage, be brave and allow all those things that have upset you in the past to be diluted by the love that is within you, that of the spirit. Then you cannot fail but to move on, to feel happier, to feel more at one with yourself and God. And then you will find true happiness; your thoughts will help you to see how much you have achieved, if you allow that positive thinking to set you free from fear of the unknown. The days ahead, of course, are unknown, but it does not matter, for you have everything you need to take on board life. The life that you are to live, for an allotted time within your physical body, to be within the physical world. There are many that have been able to show the gifts of the spirit that have led people into that greater understanding of life being eternal.

So, take up arms, my friends, not to fight with yourself or with others, but to allow the spirit to ignite within you, the power that you need to fulfil your destiny within your world. And so, we leave with you, my friends, the power of love, the power of your own mind. and you cannot fail but to understand the truth, that there is no death, that the lives of all continue.

And so, we say to you, good night and God bless.

GOOD EVENING to you, my friends, it is a pleasure to come and to talk with you.

And to help you along life's pathway, that can be arduous at times and difficult to cope with also. For, you know, when you walk the material pathway, then you have many decisions to make. You have many people that link with you, that have responsibility for you, and you for them, at different stages in your life. For you come into the world as a helpless individual, as a baby. And you are reliant on those around you to give their love and support in any way that they can. And then you go through life learning. You have to go to school, which is not always a pleasant experience, but you know, life is indeed a school room for you to bring forward knowledge and understanding of who you are and why you are living the life that you are. For you all have choices to make, and sometimes just making a choice can be difficult enough.

Today, in the Christian religion, Whit Sunday is being celebrated and remembered. For it was in the Bible that they tell you that this is when the power of the spirit manifested itself within the disciples of Jesus, and he passed on his knowledge to them, and then they had to work with the power of their own spirit to take out the Christian message. For it was apparent, you know, at Easter time, they celebrated the resurrection of Jesus, and so you see it is all telling to those that are willing to study religion and religious philosophy, that there is no death and the power of the spirit manifests through each one of you within the material world.

You all have, you see, gifts of the spirit; you all have

within you a power to move yourself forward in life. The material pathway and the spiritual pathway should run parallel, one with the other, and the more questions you have answered, the more questions you want answered. For your knowledge will increase. You know you can have knowledge from books, the Bible just being one. But you also can gain knowledge from life. Because, you know, when you think about things, there seems to be an unfairness most of the time. Whereas, in fact, it is part of the truth that you have to learn. That you have to live your life as best as you can, taking your own personal responsibility for what you do, and indeed for what you do not do, because, as we said, you have choices to make all of the time. You may need support from others that is often very necessary, and that is why we in the spirit world, whether you understand the spirit world or not, supports you in all that you do. So you are not walking the pathway within the physical world alone. It may seem so at times, but there are many that you can call upon for support, whether that is family, or friends, or institutions. It does not matter where you find the support from, but you will also find the spirit within supports you always.

It can be disappointing when you have made plans and they do materialise as you would wish, but sometimes what you are planning may not come to fruition because the timing is not right for you, and then you are forced to turn a corner and change your direction, which will be very fruitful as you continue to walk in the right direction for you. The spirit within, the real you, that is on the earth to learn lessons, to gather knowledge and to assist others, for it is giving of yourself that will help you to realise who and what you are, and you do not have to stick to creed or dogma, for each of you has what we would term freewill. The choice is yours. You know, sometimes when we have too many choices, then we cannot make our minds up.

One of the principles within Spiritualism is that of Personal Responsibility, which we have just spoken about, and there is another that talks about retribution and compensation for all the good and not so good deeds done on earth. You know, when you move on into the spirit realms of life, when the physical body ceases to house your spirit, then there is not somebody waiting for you to tell you where you went wrong, or where you went right, but you review all your actions. You review your life and then you realise where you have to make amends. Many people in your world are headstrong to say the least. You have those of different personalities; some may be a little timid, some may be a little withdrawn, but you all have a purpose in your life: to progress to ask questions, to find answers and to live your life the best way that you can. And in so doing, in giving of yourself, you are giving of the spirit that you are. And sometimes, you know, people need help. They need perhaps a listening ear, a friendly smile, or just a helping hand, because you never know anyone else's circumstances.

Each one of us will have problems, that is guaranteed. And another guarantee, of course, is that you are going to face what you term death, what we term rebirth. That is a definite. There is not much in life which is definite, because sometimes everything seems to be a chance. A chance meeting, a chance loss; you use that word in your world frequently. But you know, we have what we term a plan of action, to allow people to become aware of the spirit within themselves and the spirituality that is there within, waiting for expression.

And so it is, that we would urge you to look within to your own gifts, to your own understanding of life. You have, all of you, a thinking mind that you can use for your benefit. Sometimes, you know, your logical mind will try and play tricks on you and work overtime, and will not let you have peace of mind because of the problems you are dealing with, or others are dealing with and you are trying to support. Life in your world can be very complicated from time to time, but you have to look towards that power within you, the power that comes from God the Father.

If you go to look at others and you have help, you are very grateful indeed. We in the spirit world are very grateful also. When you begin to see the light of the truth that there is no death, that everyone will move on and move forward from the physical existence to that existence within the spirit realms of life, that world beyond matter is talked about in many religions and we talk about also, because we want to give you that hope. We want to share with you that love that comes from the Creator.

You know, sometimes you give your love unconditionally to your animals that you consider to be your pets. You give unconditional love to others around you without even realising what it is that you are doing. And so, we want to bring realisation to you. We want to tell to you that no one, whatever their belief system was, is lost. They are all alive and well in those worlds beyond that you call the realm of life. So be joyful. Know that you do indeed have to grieve at the loss of your loved ones and friends, but it is only momentary in the greater scheme of things. We ask that you pick yourself up in the knowing that they have gone on before you, and that means that you can meet again, if that is the desire.

Many people, you know, do not always wish to contact you, but that does not mean that they do not love you; they are just having to learn how to communicate with you when they no longer have a physical form. There is much to learn within our world, and many are spellbound, you might say, when they arrive at a place and realise that their life continues. It is a great revelation to many, for not many want to look into the matter of what you would term life after death, and we term continual existence of the human soul.

So, with that message that there is no death, then that must stir within you the way forward. For many are in turmoil within their mind. Many have physical problems within their own bodies, and life seems to get difficult as that physical body ages with time. But you know, that is not the end, it is but the beginning. We call it rebirth, as we have said.

And so this message needs to go out and about. There is no, what shall we say, pressure on you to unfold your own spiritual gifts, but you will feel that it is good to do so for you will feel much stronger in yourself in facing the traumas, the trials, the tribulations of life in general; and so we wish you to find great peace within your searching for understanding of your own spiritual self, and when you find peace, you find harmony and then you share your love with others and you help them also. And so, you see, you move forward, your knowledge expands. Your understanding expands, and you begin to feel that life is indeed good that you have found the key to understanding yourself, and in so doing understanding others. And so, we say to you, look to that power within and move forward slowly but conscientiously in your knowledge that death is but new life and rebirth.

And we say to you, my friends, good night and God bless.

SUNDAY 16TH AUGUST 2015

GOOD EVENING to you, my friends, it is a pleasure to come and to talk with you.

And to give you that inspiration that you may be looking for as you ask many questions within your mind, and that is why we spoke earlier of thoughts and how important it is that you take notice of what you are thinking, and indeed of what you are feeling, because, you know, sometimes when somebody may speak to you and maybe not in a kind way, you can be devastated by the feeling that has come with those words.

You see, we all interact one with the other as you walk along life's pathway. But you know, there are those in the spirit world that also walk with you. It is very important to understand that there is indeed life after death. That life continues. That the spirit that you are will move forward and onwards in life. It is you in your world of matter that happen to think, more often or not, that death is the end of the journey. Well, yes, death is the end of the physical journey, but it is not the end of the spiritual journey that your spirit, your true self, is making. And whilst you are in the physical form of the body, then your spirit is a little bit inhibited, to say the least.

In your world there is much death and destruction, and there is much before your very eyes that is brought to you through the media that brings into your mind thoughts of doom and gloom. And not necessarily thoughts of life continuing after that point that you call death, that we call transition from one state of awareness to another.

And so it is that you every day live with your own

thoughts. And believe it or believe it not, nobody can read your mind. You are in total control of your mind, and it is, what shall we say, not an easy task, because sometimes you know your mind will run away with you, especially when you are feeling a little down in the dumps, shall we say, then everything is not good. Everything is a bother; everything is troublesome, especially when you are facing your own grief for those that you have loved, that have departed from the physical world of life.

And so, you have to be able to have time to bring your thoughts back into positivity, and many without any religious belief system will instinctively say that their loved one has moved on in life, and they feel very often that presence around and about. Many people just think that that personality that has moved on in life is there to assist them, has not disappeared from their life and their memories; their thoughts keep them going when they are able to remember the good times that they had with that personality, be it a member of the family or a close friend. There is still something that keeps your mind active in wishing them well as they have departed the physical life. Many, you know, want to have a good send off, more often than not.

And it is a good idea that you do not dwell on the fact of the loss but think about the continuous existence as being a truth. A given, you might say, it does not matter what belief system you may have followed, or you may have followed none at all, because the spirit will automatically transform and transcend the vibrations of the earth into that life anew. Too many people, you know, cannot get over the grief and the loss of the physical part that is so real in the physical world. But when you open your mind and your heart and your spirit, then you can indeed feel that you have understood a little bit more of what life is about.

We are all influenced, you know, by one another. If it is not by somebody's words, it can be by somebody's actions, and sometimes, you know, people are bereft at the loss of their loved one, and it is difficult to understand the changes that have to take place when the partner, the child, has been, as you would say, lost.

Life in the physical world is not easy, but we tell to you that everybody that has spirit within, which includes the animal kingdom and indeed the kingdom of nature itself, things transform, and change is constant. You may have good memories of when you were growing up, you may have not so good memories of when you were growing up, but you all interact with others that are close to you for whatever reason. You have to make decisions, you have to be your own person, and that is all called, in your world, growing up.

And you know, it is difficult as an adult to perhaps change your ways of thinking, but you know, you have to pursue that spirit that is within you, the guidance that you have, the intuition that you feel. How many of you can say that, when you go against what you are feeling, then things start to fall apart? You have to be honest with yourself. You have to find that strength from within yourself, and it is God the Creator that has put within you that spirit. And you know, despite all the trauma within your world, many are fleeing from the oppression where there is not freedom of expression, and within your world you have man fighting man.

You may have just celebrated the fact that it was seventy years ago that the Second World War ended, and yet you look around, through your media, to see that everyone seems to be fighting everyone else. You see, you want to have an association with others, but you also want to be in charge of others. You have to sometimes be in charge of a child, or somebody that is vulnerable in one way or another, and yet the only thing you can be in charge of is yourself. You are responsible for your own actions.

You too can sometimes change your thought pattern, as was said in the reading, through meditation, through sitting in the peace and quiet of yourself. Not many in this world have much time to find the peace and quiet, but you have come here; for a moment or two, you can find that peace, that quietness, not particularly within the building but within yourself. But there are many vibrations within this building that would build up that peace, that quiet, that you are seeking and give you pointers along the way.

And so then, you see, when you find strength within, then you can go about God's work, showing to others through your actions that you have this understanding of life after death. If many people understood that, then, although they would have to go through the grieving process of that physical loss, they will be helped along the way, because they will know that their loved one is continuing life but only in a different dimension. It is important, therefore, that we do send out thoughts out to God the Creator to bring peace, to bring healing to this world, because when we send out our thoughts for others, then the spirit world draw close to us and give us that encouragement to use our spirituality in our day to day living.

You may be able to read many different holy books that will show you the way, for Jesus came to bring the light to the world, the light of understanding of the spiritual aspect of mankind. It is important, therefore, that we do, from time to time, take a step back from the rat race of life to sit quietly, to take notice of our thoughts, to help others by sending those thoughts out and asking God and the spirit realm for help.

Not one question is left unanswered, you know, but the more questions that you have answered, the more questions that there are to ask. For life is but continuous. It may be beyond understanding, some of the truths of the spirit, but we are all here on the earth vibration to learn, to learn about ourselves, to learn about the essence of who and what we are. It is the spirit within you that gives you that life, and it is the spirit within you that will move you forward, as you move forward in life and take with you that growing understanding that there is no death.

We all have to adapt to many changes in life, and one big adaptation is that of wondering how we are going to manage without that loved one that we feel part of. It is good, therefore, to seek answers to questions, and it is good that we are able, from time to time, to speak to you from those realms of light. To encourage you, to give you that confidence in your own abilities, to give you that strength, because you all have strong characters, you know, but some are more willing than others to show the strength of their character, to show the strength of their spirit. And you know, just to show one kindness to another is doing God's work, and bringing that love from the realms of the spirit into the realms of the material world. It happens all over your world that people show compassion to another and help them when they are at their lowest ebb.

And so, remember that you can always turn your thoughts to the highest, to that of the Creator, to bring you guidance, to bring you love, so that you are never alone in your journey through life, particularly when you are living in the physical world. And so, we say to you, my friends, your thoughts are important to us and to you.

And we say to you, my friends, good night and God bless.

GOOD EVENING to you, my friends, it is a pleasure to come and to talk with you.

And to tell to you, yet again, that there is indeed a Divine Plan that comes from that Great Spirit that you call God the Creator of all life. But in your world of matter, you may not give a thought to the fact that there is this Divine Plan. A plan of action. Your world will not be changed suddenly. Your world has to go through its own evolution, as do the people that dwell therein – that is, you, the spirit person that you are, that has taken on the physical body to live within the physical world, and so you are journeying in that physical world. Trying to understand life, what you are doing, why this is happening or why that. Because, you know, life doesn't go according to your own plan, for each one of you has plans throughout your life, because you are forward thinking, because you devote yourself to other people, as you go through your life trying to help, support, encourage them to be part of your life. Not just a life within the physical world, but the life that is beyond that of matter.

You see, it is the spirit that you are that links you together with those that were spirit also but have left behind their physical body and moved on in their life into the realms of spirit. It is important, therefore, that you realise the continuity of life is indeed an existence that does not end, for it is, what you would term, eternal. Now, that is very difficult to take on board, that life does not end when you all see death as the end of life. As, in fact, death is but a rebirth of that spiritual essence that you are.

And so it is that you should be encouraged to understand your spiritual self. The self that will carry you forward in life. It may sound a little difficult, but it is something that is natural, you see, life and rebirth within the seasons, within your world. And you can see at this time that the daylight is shortening, that you will be entering that time of winter, going through autumn, through winter into spring and back into summer. They are the seasons within your world, and yet, you know, so does your spirit go through many seasons in life and that life continues. Whether you understand it or not, you have elected to allow that spirit to be confined within the physical body, to live a life that is dutiful to the spirit, to that figurehead that you call God, the Great Spirit. You are doing the duty of the Great Spirit; you are the ambassador within the world of matter. So it is important that you take heed.

Sometimes, you know, people do not give a thought that the spirit lives on. And they are bereft in their grief at the loss of their loved ones and friends. Because they feel that they are left alone, and that is not altogether the truth of the matter. There are those in the spirit world, as was said in the reading, that have chosen to walk with you in your material life, albeit that they are unseen to you and to many. And they do this work out of duty, so that you may return back to the spirit having accomplished a great deal in your life, because whether you understand it or not, you give love out to others unconditionally.

You may see in your world that it seems to be torn apart by turmoil, by war, by famine, by natural disasters, and everything seems to be difficult for one and the other. But there are too many that fail to understand that the physical life is but a short span, when you think of things and life as being an eternity with which to progress.

It is important, therefore, that you do understand the principles of the Fatherhood of God and the Brotherhood of Man, because within your earthly life there are many things that you look for that keep you apart from others. You differ – the colour of your skin, in the language that you speak – and yet the essence of humankind is the spirit, and it is the spirit that should be uppermost in your mind, in your thinking. It is very important, you know, those that have moved on through that veil of death have an opportunity to communicate with you, and you do not always need a medium to bring forward that communication, for each one of you has your own way, your own method of communicating with the spirit world, albeit that you perhaps ignore those communications that are brought forward for you in your dream state and in your waking, thinking mind. So it is important that you understand your spiritual essence.

It is very important that you are not caught up in greed and dogma. It is important that you look at things through your own eyes. It is important that you are not blinded by the drudgery of life and by all the turmoil that you see in your world. There is, as we said, a Divine Plan. So do not allow fear to come into your life. Look for all that is good and then your spirit will be able to guide you forward in life. And yes, Paul was converted on the road to Damascus after he had lived a life of persecution for those that believed in the power of the spirit. And then he saw the error of his ways, and so it is when you link with that spirit within that you see the error of your ways and try to live a fulfilling life, linking to that love that comes unconditionally to you, the individual. That should give you courage, that should give you strength, and more importantly that should bring to you a great of deal of peace and love that you may pass on to others that may be ignorant of the truth that there is no death. That there is a Continuous Existence of the Human Soul. It is another of the principles set out within Spiritualism.

So, do not be afraid of the unknown, because the spirit within will guide you forward. It does not matter what religion you may follow; you will all make your transition from the world of matter to that of spirit, whatever your belief system may be. So, therefore, it is important that we tell to you of the Divine Plan so that you know that you are moving forward in your life. Physical age does not matter, but you go through that life encountering many difficulties, many changes to your life, to yourself, the physical person that you are.

So, please take forward the idea of the Divine Plan, which is unfolding, maybe slowly, but nevertheless unfolding as it should. For you are but children of the universe, and it is good that you are seeking answers to questions that you have as you face, from time to time, the loss of those that you love; but it is indeed only the physical loss, for they journey with you, to help you, to encourage you and sometimes even to advise you. But you know, you do not take kindly, as a human being, to taking any advice from another human being, and so it is that they come forward from the spirit world, but you do not have to take advice, for they do not control your life. You are in control, and that is why the principle of Personal Responsibility is important too. Know also that the laws of the spirit are different to the laws of your land. That is why you have a principle of compensation and retribution for all the good and not so good deeds done on the earth, while you are in the physical realm of life. That is not meant to put fear within you, my friends; it is meant just to assure you that what you do, and why you do it, in this life is very important, for it allows you to take that responsibility for yourself. You may support others, but you are not responsible for others. You are responsible just only for yourself.

So, that should take some of the burdens from your shoulders, and we would invite you, all of you, to link with that spirit, to find your pathway along that spiritual enlightenment that is there for you, each one of you a better understanding of who you are and why you are living within the confines of matter. Each one of you has much to offer to another and much to offer to the Great Spirit, to that Creator that you call God.

And so, we would wish you well, my friends, on your journey through life, and give you that courage and strength to go forward with hope, with strength and, more importantly, with peace.

And we say to you, my friends, good night and God bless.

GOOD EVENING to you, my friends, it is a pleasure to come and to talk with you.

And yes, perhaps, to try and bring to you that commodity that we call, all of the time, we talk about, and that is love. We call upon you, the individual, to use your own essence of self, which is spirit, which is love incarnate.

You see, you know, when you have these people that become discarnate beings, because they have left your world of matter, they do not suddenly become angelic in our world. They see the results of their actions, they see the results of their words, and they see the results of their life that has gone before in that realm of the material world. And so, you see, it is all a process of learning. It all a process of understanding about the spirit that you are. Not about the spirit that you will become. So you see, it is very important that you do understand that your life will continue after that point that you call death. We tell this to you all of the time because it is the essence, you see. It is the essence of what it is that we have to tell to you.

Because there is much in your world that causes, what shall we say, great fear amongst the human race. Because everybody seems to be fighting for recognition of their beliefs, of their understanding, and yet, you know, that cannot be allowed to happen, and your world be no more, because that seems to be what many think is inevitable, for your world of matter that you call earth. It is a learning ground, you know, and so it is that you must use your mind. You must allow common sense to prevail, because, you see, with your sensitivity of the spirit, then you do at times feel bombarded by life. Not necessarily what is happening in distant, far lands, but what is happening within your very own life. Because you all have a life to live.

And maybe on the news reels you have heard of people that have had, what shall we say, narrowly escaped being injured or killed in the atrocities that have been filling your news time. And you would think, would you not, that there was no other news to deliver, because they keep telling you the same things that are happening in just one small part of your world. And so, you become saturated with negativity as you listen, as you watch, as your mind tries to make sense of what is happening in your world. It does not matter how many accounts that you hear from those that were there, you still cannot manage to understand how you would feel in those same circumstances.

Only a short time ago, about a week, everybody was focussed on Remembrance Day, or Remembrance Sunday, and then the last week Remembrance Day itself; those that lost their lives fighting for freedom throughout the ages, not just in the two main world wars, because, you know, today through your TV screens it would seem that everyone seems to be at war with everyone else.

And so, again, you have two contrasts there. And it is important that you do seek peace, but you have to seek that peace from within yourself. You will not find it outside of yourself. But if you can find it within yourself, and everyone could do the same, then your earthly world would be transformed. People would not be brainwashed into believing something that is not true.

It does not matter what you believe or who you follow; your spirit is going to transcend the world of matter at that point that you call death.

So again, I am repeating this because it is so important: if you come into your own world of life to what you experience day to day, you will know that you have your own communication with those that have passed on that were dear and beloved to you. It is not something that is supernatural, as you would be led to believe by your media, that, what do you say, put hype on such things.

And it is, therefore, important that you begin to understand how your spirit within you, the essence of you, is communicating with you. You do not need to go to lessons, shall we say; it is the lessons of daily life that bring you to that awareness that you are more than skin and bone, with a brain that has a logical mind; because, sometimes, you know, you defy all logic because you have a feeling within you, that you need to be doing this or that, or you do not need to go to this place or that place, and it is not easily explained by coincidence because, you know, you are very sensitive to that spirit that is the real you. It is unfortunate, you know, that there are so many within your world that would wish to have control over you. You may think that there are many within our world that would wish to have control over you, but my friends, you are in control.

We may have a little control over our medium here, to speak these words, but that is because we have a partnership in being, you know, where we have permission from our channel to come as close as we can to allow you to feel the power of the spirit as we talk individually to you and your own spirit. So that you may find peace, that you may find answers to questions, that you may find out about things that are going to help you in your day to day living to have more faith, to have more courage, to have more light within your world. For that Creator that you call God brings the light of the spirit into your world.

How many have been called to prayers in the last two days to help those that have lost their physical lives, so that they become aware of their new being, their new place of residence. It may all seem sudden, but those in the spirit world that connect to each individual human being would have been there to greet them and to make them feel at peace with themselves. It does not matter who has done what to who. Everyone will be greeted and told of their new life that is there ahead of them, and what they have to do to make amends for, what it is that they have been trying to do in the lives that they have led. What is important is that the life of each individual will continue. There will be halls of healing and learning so that those that do not understand their new abode will be able to learn quickly, and will then try their very best to begin their journey, one of enlightenment so that they come out of the darkness and into the light of God's love.

So, my friends, we ask you to banish all fear that you have in your mind, that you look within for the positivity for the strength and for the understanding that you need, so that you know that you are going to have a life that will be what you want it to be, that you have control over your own self. It may seem daunting to take that stand, but it is important that you realise that you are not controlled by anyone or anything, but you have your own motives for what you do and what you do not do in life. Share what you have with others, and others will share with you. That is the beginning of giving of yourself in service to God the Creator, and then you will find everlasting peace, and then if every individual can manage to find that peace, then your world will be transformed. It may take eons of time before that knowledge comes to one and all, but rest assured that we in the spirit world are working tirelessly to bring that light, to dispel darkness and fear.

So, take up the challenge to look for peace within yourself, and you will see how that transforms your understanding of life. Your sensitivity might be great, but in that knowledge you will become strong in yourself, ready to face any challenge, any adversity, and so it is that we leave with you peace and the love that comes unconditionally from the Creator that you call God.

And we say to you, my friends, good night and God bless.

Chapter Six
Port Talbot SNU Church, Port Talbot

SUNDAY 11TH MARCH 2012

GOOD EVENING to you, my friends, it is a pleasure to come and to talk with you.

And to impart to you words that may make you think a little deeper about life, and in particular your lives, your individual life, that you are. Because as you have just sung, in that hymn, you will live forever, for an eternity. Your life will not end at that point of physical death. Because the spirit will move on, into that world of spirit, that world of light, and you will be encouraged towards progression to the Godhead, the Father.

But when we have an opportunity to speak to you, in this way, we would bring that encouragement to you now for you to look within for your own spiritual attributes, so that you may make a difference, firstly, to your life and, secondly, to the lives of others by leading by example. Because you are all channels for that spirit world and for the spirit that is you, the essence of yourself, and so it is that you can take time to link with that spirit, because all of you will be looking for harmony within your life, in your spiritual life and in your material life also. For the paths will always run parallel, one with the other.

And when you have an understanding that your spirit is going to live forever, then you will be able to enjoy your material existence, for you should not worry in the same way, you should not grieve in the same way, if you understand the truth of the matter: that you spirit will live on and so does the spirit of everything and everyone, because the energy that is the spirit will always transform and work its way towards the light. And so, we should dispel all darkness and fear that is within the minds of mankind. Because there is great conflict within your world, and there can also be conflict within yourselves, but you all know, if you listen to your intuitive self, what is right and what is wrong for you, the individual.

So, we would encourage you to question the spirit world, so that you can learn, because the lessons within the physical existence can be very difficult at times, as was mentioned in that reading, but you need to find ways in which you can cope, and you will realise that the spirit world and what you find within yourself can only assist you, can only support you, in your everyday dealings with other people. There is too much criticism within your world.

If you look around you at this time, now, nature is bursting into life, although things have looked dead and beyond repair, and so it is that sometimes you live in the material world and your spirit appears to be dead and beyond repair, because you do not listen to the promptings of your spirit within you, within your very being. And so, we would ask you to take note. We would ask you to look at all the blessings bestowed upon you from God the Father, and to be thankful for those blessings and to give thanks to the Creator that you call God. In following just those ideas you will feel much happier within yourself.

We do not want you to take everything for granted, which seems to be the way within your modern world. People have many things because they are always wanting, but it is your needs that are met by God and not necessarily your wants, because there is a subtle difference, you see, between the two, and all that we ask of you is that you give a little thought to what you are about, to what you are doing with your life.

Just listening to one or two comments, at the beginning of this service, all of you are busy, very busy, with life. And sometimes you get carried away on the crest of the materialism wave, to forget about the message within Spiritualism. It may sound a little harsh as to what we are saying to you, but we are only wanting you to make sense of life. When you read the newspapers do you take everything on board of being the truth? I do not think so, and so it is with your quest for knowledge of the spirit world; we would not wish you to take everything as the truth. As has been said, you should be asking questions, you should be testing the spirit world, and you should be taking forward guidance that you feel is right for you. Because as time progresses and the more questions you have answered, the more questions you will have until you become knowledgeable about the spirit world, knowledgeable about those that would come to you to give you their communication, to say their hello.

You all rely a lot, do you not, on that gadget called a mobile phone, because you are asked to switch it off for a short time. You are always getting messages or communicating verbally with somebody else using that gadget, but you know, if you take time you can communicate with those guides and helpers that walk with you. You can be inspired along the way, so that you are doing God's work, that you are being of service to others.

There are many that develop their gifts of the spirit. There are many within this environment of this church that use and give freely of their gifts from the spirit world. They do the laying on of hands, they send out healing through thought, they allow communication in the way of clairvoyance and mediumship to be available to all those that walk through the doors of this establishment, and we in the spirit world take every opportunity that we can to work with those that are going to open their minds and work as a channel for the spirit world. So we do not want you to shut the doors of opportunity that are there for each one, although in your material world sometimes the doors seem to shut tight, and there seems to be no way forward for opportunity, but you know, there always is a way forward. You cannot go back over the years.

You can learn from your experiences, but you have to push forward and onward and accept what has happened in the past. Lessons for you to learn. Lessons for you to understand. We would not expect you to go back to school, in the infants' class, if you are already up to university standard; all that we would ask is that you use the intelligence that you have, and you will be lead forward in the correct way. Do not go into that 'poor me' syndrome or 'why me', because the answer is 'why not'. You have all that you need within you, to help you, to give you that strength so that you can pull yourself up and move on, and in so doing be an inspiration to others that are perhaps not as courageous as you.

Just by being here, at this time, you have decided to look into those things that would be classed as unseen, allowing yourself to be fed by the essence of the spirit within you. You may all want communication from certain individuals in the spirit realm, but all that we can do is to aid you in your quest. So we ask that you do not give up when the going gets a little difficult, but that you look within yourself and around and about you for the help that is on offer from those realms unseen.

Many of you will understand that you have come a long way since you first stumbled across the idea that life is continuous, that there is no death, because, you know, when you think about it, things do not make sense if the end of life was that of the physical existence. And so, we congratulate you all thus far on your endeavours, and we would give you that peace, that love that comes from God, so that you can find harmony within, so that you are not fighting between the material and the spiritual aspects, that you can dovetail it in altogether, for there are many books that have been written that will show the way forward, because there have been those Masters that have come to the earth and walked within the light of the spirit, and their spirituality, has not gone unnoticed so to speak.

You may think that there are many religions within your world that have a fanatical element to them, but that is because they have not found balance and harmony within their mind and within their spiritual attributes, and so we come back to that word of harmony, and we would give you that to think on, for a little while, because, you know, when things are harmonious within your life, you immediately feel better, but worry can put harmony to one side, and then everything is in turmoil.

And so, we would ask that you do not worry so much, that you take everything to God in prayer, and that will help because that is linking with the Godhead so that you can work out for yourselves that you have to do some thinking. That you have to do some analysing of who and what you are. It is not difficult, and this is only advice. You can take it or leave it. But you will benefit greatly if you take it. And if you can find harmony and live in harmony, firstly with yourself, then you will be able to live in harmony with others, and that is good, that means that the spirit is always alive and well and working with mankind to bring to your earth, peace and tranquillity, for it is the love of God the Father that will aid in this quest. But things have to start within oneself, and that is why we would remind of that principle of Personal Responsibility. There are no creeds that should divide, for the spirit should unite one and all in your world. So, use those gifts wisely and acknowledge the strength and the power that your own spirit gives you, daily, to tackle life within the physical world.

And so, we say to you, my friends, good night and God bless.

SUNDAY 18TH MARCH 2012

GOOD EVENING to you, my friends, I am back again, so soon, yes, in your time, but you know it is important that you understand that the spirit world do not really go away; all of you have your helpers, inspirers and those that walk with you through your earthly life; whether you acknowledge them or not does not really matter as long as you search for answers to your questions so that life begins to make sense to you.

The word that we chose to read tonight was that of 'Love', which in your world can be misunderstood, misconstrued however you would wish to see it. Because, you know, today you have been celebrating what you term 'mothers' day', and all of you understand that great love bond that there is between mothers and children, not forgetting, of course, fathers and children, because that is what you become in life for some of you, parents, and as time progresses you do not only have children, but you have grandchildren, great grandchildren, and so the generations go on and on and on, and life in your world continues. As does life in our world, you know, because there is continuity of the spirit, for at that point you call death, your spirit will move forward into the spirit world, and all those that are tied to you through the ties of love will be there to assist, and those left on the earth plane also, you are tied to them through that bond of love. And you know that God the Creator gives unconditional love to one and all. And as you journey through your physical life, you are always searching for being able to show your love to another. But when you show your love in an unconditional fashion, that is true love. There are no confines to that; it is not power over somebody that is necessary, it is just this giving of yourself allows you to feel the benefit of that spirit within, so that you feel complete, that you feel strengthened, uplifted and aided along your way in life, because it is arduous within the material world.

And one hard lesson to learn is that you cannot have all that you want. But you can have all that you need, for there is much difference between want and need. And you know, in your world you see things through the media that some do not even have what they need to sustain their life in the physical sense, and you see horrific scenes, do you not, of starving children, for instance, and you feel helpless to help them and others that are suffering in your world. But you know, when you understand that death is nothing at all, but just a transition for the spirit of the individual, then things make a little more sense within one's own mind, and so you see, it should help those that grieve at the loss of their loved ones, because age is no respecter of when that spirit is going to move on in life. Because that is the truth, and there are many things that have to be learnt and understood, but rest assured, as your principles say, that God is the Father, Creator of all life, and you see that love of God is given to one and all, unconditionally, without any strings attached, to use a modern phrase.

So do not think of love as all hearts and flowers, because, you know, sometimes to give of yourself is far more meaningful than to buy expensive gifts and to call at the door of someone just on a certain day that is named to honour, as today is that of motherhood. It is very easy to put labels on many things, but you know, you can only do your best in your life and work within the circumstances that may confine you. Because in your world personalities clash with personalities, and life can become difficult, however much you would love another. For in your world, it would seem that there is more disruption within family life these days than in the past, but there has always been disruption if you look back over generations. And so it is that you have to come to terms with the traumas and difficulties of life. We cannot take those away from you, but we can give you courage, strength and understanding so that life becomes a little happier for you, because the peace and the love of the spirit is found within each one of you. You all have that spiritual essence; whether you understand it or not, it is there for you, to work with, for you to change things for the better, if that is your desire. Because there are too many in your world that you may term troublemakers, and we would endeavour to encourage the peacemakers because, you know, sometimes just because personalities clash, or one wants power over another, then there becomes great trauma that is really needless and sometimes useless.

And so, we want to put the idea into your minds that you are all encompassing of that spirit within, that is going to move you forward, that is going to give you understanding about the spiritual truths. You talk in your principles about the Brotherhood of Man, which symbolises that you are all equal, that you are all of the spirit of the Father that you call God. It is very important that you understand that how you live your life is in accordance with the natural law. That is what we would ask of you. Because there is another principle, that is about compensation and retribution for all the good and evil deeds done on earth. That isn't a sword hanging over your head, my friends; it is just to tell you that you will be responsible for your actions, and that also comes under Personal Responsibility. You also have an eternity with which to progress towards that light of God the Father, and so you see, you are making these tiny steps forward every time that you look within at your own spiritual understanding and development of your gifts of the spirit. Each one of you is a talented individual in many and varied ways, because we cannot clone you so that you are the same as somebody else, although you are all equal in the spiritual aspirations and aspects within yourself.

So, we ask that you look to sending out your thoughts in prayer. That you sit quietly from time to time to experience that inner strength and energy that is there for you. In your modern world, you are busy, busy, busy all the time, and it is difficult to find five minutes to rest your mind from all that is happening in your day to day lives and your day to day living.

So, we are mindful of all that, but just to come into this establishment, you have taken time out from the busyness of your lives to sit and listen, to have those messages come to you from the spirit realms of those that love you and walk with you and want to encourage you to understand that there is a life beyond that of the material world, that there is much to be accomplished. That you are all precious in God's sight. None of you are lost sheep, you are all being guided, if you would but listen to that inner small voice that you may call your conscience.

And so, we would welcome all enquirers; perhaps that is the message you should put over your doorway, so that people are not afraid of the unknown, of the unseen, that they are more willing to understand that you have a natural ability within yourselves to understand many things that may be unsaid but that you know within yourself to be correct for you. Because that intuition tells you, if you are wise enough to take note of your feelings and not get carried away and fired up by what other people believe is best for you. You know what is best for you, because you are you and no one can change that, and so that is why we would give you these suggestions and a little bit of an interpretation into those seven principles that are up there on the wall. Because you can interpret them as you wish, but the whole essence of those principles is to bring you to that understanding that within you is a spiritual light that you are responsible for, to shine out into the world, and in all the devastation that you see within your media, you also see those that are willing to give of themselves, those doctors and nurses, even the reporters that put their lives at risk to show to the world what is really happening within your world. However uncomfortable that may seem, as it comes into your homes, into your lives, allow it to move that spirit on so that you can send your thoughts out to God the Creator, the source of all life and the essence.

So, it may be a little word, 'Love', but it is the essence of your spirit, because it is the essence of God. So, remember that you are powerful within yourselves. You are able to work with that spirit and to work with your gifts and to feel at peace by just having a little communication with the spirit world and those that would wish to come back to say that they still love you. That they are proud of you, that you are doing well, and when you feel that you are not doing so well they bring their encouragement to give you that peace of mind, to give that strength, to give you that help that you need, because you become enmeshed sometimes within materialism itself.

So, let us become enmeshed in Spiritualism itself. Because if you work closely with the spirit then you can move mountains, so to speak. Bring light into the lives of those that are fearful of the unknown, because they do not open their minds to the fact that their loved ones are alive and well and wanting all the time to share in that love, whether it be between the two worlds. But remember that you are willing to share love with those in the physical world, so you should too be willing to share your love with those in the spiritual world of light. And so we leave you, my friends, with the light and the love that comes in, that comes in from those that would generate the energies so that you can have communication, not only in this church but in your own being. You can all communicate with those that you know, those that you love, and you talk sometimes of the darkness in your world and feel that it cannot be improved, but it can, because the light from the spirit world will penetrate into your world as soon as individuals take on board that they are responsible for all that goes on within the physical realms.

You cannot all take on that responsibility, but you can take responsibility for yourself. You cannot take responsibility for the whole world, and of that we are quite clear. But if you just find out what is best for you, so that you can help others, then that is all that we ask, because all actions, all thoughts, should be done in love, in love that comes from God the Father, and then you will see that many will respond to that love, to that light; that is how your healing works. There is the laying on of hands, yes, but there is also absent, distant healing so you are all capable of giving a thought to another. Giving a helping hand to another, all that is working for the spirit, and as you work in love so your world will change for the better, and peace will abound within individuals, and then it will move out so that collectively things begin to change. That is what we have come to talk to you about this evening.

It has been a pleasure, and so we would say to you, my friends, good night and God bless.

GOOD EVENING to you, my friends, it is a pleasure to come and to talk with you.

And perhaps the first thing we should say to you is an apology for the length of the reading, but you know that word 'responsibility' should not have so many letters, and then it would have been shorter, yes? But you know, there should have been something in there for everyone to take from those words. And that is good, because you are all here, you know, to walk your own spiritual pathway in life. And some, you know, do not even consider anything about the spiritual realms of life, because they are totally immersed or enmeshed within the materialism of your world, and that does not make them to be not the right type of people in your world, but they are on their own mission, you see, and they do not realise until they return to our world, that they should have been looking at all things and not just the physical, material vibration of life, and so they begin to progress when they have returned to us, on our side, the other side of life, as you sometimes call it.

But you know, if you can begin to open your mind to the understanding that you are a spiritual being, then it is much easier when you make your transition, because you have already begun to investigate the world unseen, that is the realm of the spirit. And so, what can we say, it is better to have perhaps a foot in both camps, and then you can begin your search and your journey, piecing everything together like a big jigsaw because, you know, if you only function on the physical level, then I am afraid life will not make much sense to you. Because you can see that, you know, it is very fragile, your life, your physical life, because, you know that you were born into the physical body, and that you will, at some time, in your timescale of years, you will pass away, and your physical body will go back to the earth.

And then, what then, is what you should be asking yourself, and it is your responsibility, of course, to live your life how you will. We do not come forward to tell you what to do, and by the same token we do not control you; you have a thinking mind all of your own. Each one of you has that you know, and you make your decisions accordingly. And sometimes you do hesitate, because you wonder if you are doing the right or the wrong thing. And sometimes you go by what you would term your conscience. How do you know that is not your spirit within, telling you, advising you, giving you a little bit of encouragement to work as you should with your own spirit? That is, the real person that you are. And it is never too late, you know, for any of you to take responsibility for your life and your living, and what you are doing with the gifts that you have. Because there is not one of you here that does not have some sort of ability that can be used to help a) yourself and b) other people.

But you know, you do have to look at yourselves so that you can become open and be channels for the spirit world to use. How many times have you leant a listening ear, or a helping hand, to somebody else? And that has made you feel that whatever you did was worthwhile, because the person that you have given that aid to has felt better and has changed a little bit in their understanding of you. Because, you know, sometimes people do things with the wrong motivation, and that is when things start to get a little bit difficult for the individual that is doing acts without the right motivation behind it. Because you cannot control what other people are doing by your own actions and your own mind, and yet you are not here to control anyone else, just as we are not coming forward to control you in any way.

You have to take on responsibility for yourself, and that is what we need you to know. Because, then, when you understand that you have freedom, and once you have freedom, as that reading suggested, then your world will transform, and it will be a much different place to what you see today. Because, you know, there are always those that are wanting power over others, and this is what we come to say to you, that you cannot control one and all. And, you see, you have to be honest with yourselves. It is good that you question this, that and the other. And sometimes, you know, you get answers to these questions, but sometimes you do not realise that the answer has been given, because it is subtle in the way that we are able to influence you as a human being. Because how many of you have said, 'oh, that's not from the spirit world, that is just my overactive imagination'? But we work mind to mind.

Our medium here has said that she works in the trance state and allows us to speak, but we are not fully in control; we have to pass these words through her logical thinking mind, you know. And so it is all about co-operation, it's all about being sensible, it's all about taking responsibility, and that is so important to one and all. It's so easy to blame another for your transgressions, you see. And yet, when you move to our world, you will be judge and jury of your life, not anybody from the spirit world. And you will see that you have to work in making amends for those decisions that were not altogether the right decisions. But it does not matter, because every time, you know, you are moving forward in your life, every time that you do this, that or the other. And so, we want to give you encouragement to be who you truly are.

You know, you can all wear different clothes and give different impressions by how you dress, and yet, you know, we in the spirit world can see past the confines of the physical, and we know who you are, what you are, and more importantly, what you are trying to achieve. And you know, many blessings are bestowed upon your world, and yet you totally ignore some of these. You have moaned, have you not? About the terrible weather conditions over your wintertime, and you know, still nature is a kingdom all of its own, that has to have these ups and downs, that has to change, because of the circumstances that are about. There are too many things that are beyond your control as being a human individual, you see. And so, you do have the blessings of nature, because there will always be an equilibrium that is achieved, although sometimes it seems that that is unachievable And so, things change from day to day, and no doubt as you move into summer, you will be complaining of the heat and even maybe the dryness, you see, because it doesn't suit one, and all but the promptings of the spirit suits every individual, because you progress at your own rate. It does not matter what you think, what you believe but we tell to you the truth, that you cannot die, you do have an eternity with which to progress and perfect your own spirituality.

And so, that is good news, you see. Because there are many in your world that are in constant despair when they lose one loved one after another, and how many times does it happen within a family that they all 'pop off' together, and so you go from one funeral to the next, to the next, to the next, and so then you begin to lose your faith and your understanding of what it means when you reach that point that you call death, but really it is rebirth of the spirit back into the spiritual realms of light

And so, then you can see a bigger picture of all that is happening to your friends and family. And that is why we do endeavour, from time to time, to prove, through mediumship, survival of the spirit. But even that, you are given information, and you go away and make all sorts of excuses as to why it is not one hundred and one percent correct, yes? You do it all the time, my friends, you question, question, question, and we come forward and we try to help you, to give you that sense that all is not lost when you lose somebody at that point that you call death.

And so, if we could eradicate that idea that death is the end, then we would be working well, and your churches would be full and not empty. They all come to those things that are sensational, but they do not come to listen to the understanding that we have in the spirit world, slightly different to your understanding, because we want to talk about life continuing, and you want to talk death as something finished, you see.

So, we want to move you all forward, and that is

what we are interested in doing. To help you, to help you see that the strife in your life is but lessons that you have to deal with, and the more that you have to deal with then the faster that you grow in your understanding of yourself, when you realise that you are a spirit and not just one dimension as a physical body.

So, that long word, 'Responsibility'; we hope that you have taken something away with you that has answered a question or two in your mind, so that you can stick with the truth, that you cannot die, you can only move on, and that we in the spirit world enjoy being able to communicate with you. So many of you have had what you would term psychic experiences, and yet you brush them aside and forget all about them, because you want to be what you would consider to be normal. That is why it is good to get you together so that you can see the blessings that you have and look on the positive side, rather than the negative side of life. And so, we want you to go out of here feeling energised by the power of your own spirit, by the power that you have sat in, because we have to work with energy, you see, and each one of you produces energy, even if you are sat there listening to every word that is uttered.

But we do, indeed, thank you for your attention and say to you that you are able, at all times, to link with the spirit world, and that when you do, you are the ones that are inviting us to aid you, to assist you; we do not control you, my friends, but we must say to you that you are in control of you. And as soon as you take that on board, you begin to see, to expand your mind, to expand your awareness, so that you know that there is more to life than your three-dimensional world. A lot to take on board, we know, but you can read this and you can read that, as there is much to digest from books, and yet it is up to you what you want to accept and what you want to reject, and that is fine, because we want you to move forward in great strides, with great confidence, so that you can face the rigours of your earthly life with a great deal of courage, fortitude and strength.

And so, we say to you, my friends, take on that responsibility of your investigation of life and enjoy. And so, we say good evening and God bless.

GOOD EVENING to you, my friends, it is a pleasure to come and to talk with you.

And to, what shall we say, shower you with positivity. Because there is doom and gloom within your world, within your day to day living, because there are always obstacles to face and problems to sort, because, you know, your life just seems to be that way. But in all the happenings that you encounter within your life, your spirit is prepared, whether you understand that or not, it does not matter to us in the spirit world. But your spirit is there to be a help and guidance to you, the human being that you are; but you know you are a spiritual being as well, and if you do not understand, it is paramount that you look towards your spiritual self for all the answers to the questions that you may have as to live your life in the material existence. For that is only part of your life.

We have already mentioned in the prayer that your spirit will have its rebirth at that point that you call death, when the physical body is no more, when you do not need the confines of that physical frame. And so it is that your spirit is the true person that you are. Your mind and your spirit equals your soul. Because, you see, you have a logical, thinking mind that sometimes holds you back in the great scheme of things, because from the time you incarnated into the earth plane, you were learning, you had a plan, before you came to take on the physical confines.

And so it is that you have work to do. You can all be channels for the spirit world, for your own spirit to have expression, so that you will realise that you are working towards a plan, that you are indeed part of the Divine Plan of God. And that extract told you all about the fact that religions are unimportant, but you have been conditioned by religions throughout eons of time, and so to put those religious beliefs to one side and begin your own explanation and exploration for an explanation is what is important. Because you are wanting answers to questions, you are wanting to understand about the life beyond the confines of matter. And that is good, because you are questioning, you are not looking for creeds and dogma to keep you on the straight and narrow, because many religions put fear into mankind over the eons of time and centuries of life in your world.

And so it is that we break the mould, so to speak. We say yes if you wish to follow in the confines of religious beliefs. That's fine; if you want to be a solo player, shall we put it that way, and look for answers yourself, then those in the spirit world that walk with you, those family, friends, those unknown to you that have appointed themselves as guides and helpers, are indeed doing all they can to keep you on the straight and narrow.

Looking at your own self, that is not an easy task, you know, and that is why you are courageous to do so, to look at that spirit, that spirit that is going to transform and transcend your physical world. And so, you cannot fail, you see. You are going to succeed because it does not matter if you believe in an afterlife or not. You will still turn up at the appointed time, the time that is right for your spiritual self. And so, there are no, what shall we say, signposts really for you to follow, other than your own intuition, your own feelings, because you know whether you are doing something for the correct reason or not. You know when you are doing what is right for you.

You may ask advice of others, but you do not always take that advice. And that is the same with those who reside in the spirit world; they can come forward and communicate with you and pass on their advice, but it is up to you whether you take that advice or not. Because you have Personal Responsibility; it one of the principles of your Spiritualism. But you know, even when you look within the belief system of Spiritualism, there are rules and regulations that seem to carry on forever and ever.

We want you to understand that you don't have to follow an 'ism', you just have to follow the spiritual essence of who you are. Because you came with a plan, and you know, they say that if you plan that is good. If you fail to plan, then you plan to fail. But there is no failure, you know, because you do your best in your world of matter, and that is all that we ask of each one of you. And so, we want to put into you that positivity, that understanding that you can achieve, that you can help yourself and, more importantly, others.

The physical body only has a certain life's span, because that is the very nature of that body. It is going to decay; it is going to allow the spirit freedom to move back into the spiritual realms of light. In your world there are too many that seem to think that if they kill off others in the human race, in particular, then they are going to achieve, they're going to win the war, they're going to win the battle, but let's just say that there is no such thing as a winner or a loser, because all of you, in the human race, are going to end up in the same place. The body will go back to the earth, and the spirit will go back to the spirit realms, and so what are people achieving, I ask, in your world, where they just want power over others, all of the time? They want to be in charge, they want to dictate.

We in the spirit world are not allowed to dictate. That is why, as it said in the reading, there will be no blinding flash when everyone will turn to the spiritual truths to advance the cause, to bring peace into your world, to bring harmony into your world, to bring love into your world. It will be a slow process, with slow progress, but we have a Divine Plan that comes from God the Father, that is why your first principle speaks of the Fatherhood of God and also of the Brotherhood of Man, because you are all following the same plan, you are all part of the Divine Plan, and so you cannot succeed if you are ignoring the spirituality within you, the spiritual essence within you, and that is why we have found time to speak on the Divine Plan.

So, ask your questions of the spirit world, and you will get answers when the time is right for you. Take your steps forward and do your very best, and you will succeed. And so, we want you to feel the love, the peace, the harmony that comes from those that walk with you, not just one day at a time, but walk with you for an eternity of time, and therefore you cannot fail. So, please remember that all that we ask is that you do your best, that you are following the Divine Plan if you take time out to look for spiritual truths and understand spiritual values and the law of cause and effect.

And so, in essence, you make your own reality. It does not matter what is written in the books of days gone by; they may help individuals, that is true; the work of Silver Birch has been documented and helps many, and so it is that we would point you towards the written word, to help you to ease your mind, to bring in that positivity when you get down and you feel that you are down and out. But that is not the case; you are surviving; you are a survivor; you cannot die. That is a spiritual truth, my friend, that there is an eternity with which to progress, that every human soul will move on, will walk tall in the realms of light. But first, there are lessons to learn. You may not see that blinding flash, but you all have the spirit within that is your guide, that is your help, to sustain you in those times when things seem to be going awry. But we would say to you keep happy, keep positive, keep cool, keep calm and know that you are being helped every step of the way by those guides and family and friends that you would term unseen, that we would term helpers and guides to you the individual.

So, do not become disheartened when you switch on your TV set, or any other means of communication in your modern technological world. Keep positive and pass on that message, that truth, that the spirit can never die. That there is time to get over grief, that there is time to have a good time in your material world. That you are there to serve God, to serve the spirit world, and in so doing your spirit will grow and grow, and so when you return to the spirit realms, you will be understanding of all the spiritual truths.

And so, my friends, we wish you well on your journey in life, because, you know where you are heading, you know where you are going; without fail everyone will return to that spiritual essence of themselves, and so we say to you work hard, play hard and know that God is with you.

And so, we say good night and God bless.

GOOD EVENING to you, my friends, it is a pleasure to come and to talk with you.

And it is important, you know, that we do indeed talk to you about the truths of the spirit. Because, as you know, there are, indeed, many different religions that can be followed. And yet, you know, there are many that hide behind their religious belief, as they realise that they have to just follow a format and that will enable them to move on into the life beyond that of the physical.

Because, you know, in your world, you want things put there for you, perhaps something to lean upon in your times of distress, whereas, in point of fact, you should be looking within yourself, for it is the power of the spirit within you, the individual, that sustains life within you, a life that will continue, because the spirit cannot die. Indeed, the physical body has to go back to the earth. The spirit has to go back to the spiritual realms of life, beyond the confines of matter. And so, if that truth was widely understood and known, then all your religious creeds and dogmas would fall away, instantly. Your world would then become a much more peaceful place in which the humankind can live.

Because the idea is that you should all be living in harmony, one with the other. But there are so many things that divide you, one from the other; language is one thing that can divide, because if you do not understand a language, then you cannot communicate with that person, and so it is that a barrier is built up. And that is how it has been, my friends, with the religions that have built up in your world by putting different interpretations on events and things that perhaps should have been kept simple.

The truth is that when your spirit returns to our world, sometimes, you know because a person is so enmeshed whilst on the earth with religious dogma, they do not understand that they no longer live in the physical world and that life is still available to them. By that we mean that their minds are closed off, and then we have to work with them to bring them around to the understanding that they are alive and well in a different state of being. In a different state of vibration where it is a world of thought.

And so your thoughts of your everyday mind can hinder you if you do not allow yourself to go by that spirit that is within you and use your own intuition about what it is that you are willing to believe. You all have logical, thinking minds, and we ask you to use that mind of yours. Because it is something that you have to utilise; you have to learn when you are children your ABC in order that you can communicate and that you can read and others things that you have to do to conform with what is required of you within your society, within your world. But you all have gifts of the spirit, and you all have the ability to be channels for the spirit world. But you have to have faith in that spirit that is the real you. It is a natural occurrence, of course, for your spirit to be released from your body when you reach that point that you call death, and then, you know, you should understand all about the purpose of your life within the physical world.

For you all come to the world of matter in order to fulfil your spirit, in order to fulfil that ambition that you have to enable your spirit to be refined by the lessons that you are learning along life's material pathway. And so it is that many do not look into those things unseen, into that world unseen. And yet it is a natural occurrence, this transition from one state of vibration to another. And so we would, indeed, help you to understand this truth. So that you can help others that are distressed and upset when they lose loved ones and friends in the physical form. Nothing can stop that event happening. But it happens at the right time for the soul that you are. And so it is that you live your life as best as you can. Being of service to others, that is the simple truth. And all that we ask of you.

There is no need for ritual; there is no need for understanding every word that has been written by those theologians of years gone by. Indeed, there have been many that have come to show the way, shown their light that the spirit is, and encouraged others to follow in that understanding of spiritual unfoldment. So there is much to learn, we understand that, but we tell to you that it is best to keep things as simple as you can.

You may have great minds, many of humankind have, that seem to be able to tap into this, that and the next thing, to bring about strides forward in medical science, and in enabling the medical profession to extend life, to extend it for longer than was some years back. It is what you call progress, but we say to you, my friends, is it progress? Because, you know, sometimes you perhaps need to live a longer time to fulfil your mission, to fulfil the Divine Plan that you are going to help others along life's pathway, and in so doing, help yourself. And so, we would remind you that religion does not matter. What matters to the spirit world is how you live and how you work for the betterment of oneself and the betterment of others. It is no good putting yourself on a pedestal and saying, well, I'm okay up here and you are down there not understanding life at all. You must share.

You are indeed, coming to that time when many celebrate the harvest time. And yet, you know, as you are able in this country to gather in the crops to sustain physical life, there are many that do not have enough food to eat. And so, it is all about, my friends: caring and sharing. But you know, it is important that you go by that very person that you are, that you do look for the power of the spirit, that you then try your very best to be of service to God the Father, the Great Spirit, the giver of all Life. There will always be ups and downs in life, that is for sure. But it does not mean that you cannot surmount these obstacles in your life, and in so doing become stronger in your resolve that you are spirit here and now, and that there is no death. That is the simple truth, my friends, so go and tell others of your understanding of life. Not just life in the physical, material world, but life beyond the confines of matter. This will give people food for thought. Just as you have to have food, as we have said, to sustain the physical, you also have to have food to sustain the spiritual aspect of yourself. So, take heart, take heed, and move forward, and give out that message of life eternal and eternal love being given to all from God the Father.

We say to you, my friends, good night and God bless.

GOOD EVENING to you, my friends, it is a pleasure to come and to talk with you.

And you know, that reading may have been a little bit lengthy, and had our channel chosen the reading, she might have given you the first one in the book because it is short, you see. And you know, sometimes it is difficult to keep concentration for any length of time, you know, and it takes you back, no doubt, to those school days when you got bored with what the teacher was saying to you, yes? (*Congregation: Yes*)

But nevertheless, you all learnt and you are all learning to this day about life, my friends. And it can arduous, and it can be difficult, and that is why you are here to get a little bit of help along the way; help from within yourselves, of course, because you all have a spirit within you that is strong. How many times have you seen that happen to your loved ones; their spirit shines through the physical ailments that they have, and you think they are going to get well again, and then suddenly they have moved on in their life and moved to the spirit realms? So, you see, that was the spirit getting ready for its continued journey in life. We do not like to use the word dead, you know, and yet many think of Spiritualists as talking to the dead. Yes? (*Congregation: Yes*). But you know, we are very much alive, you see, but in a different state of vibration, and as was said in that reading, you know, there are very many different states, and the physical life is one that is heavy and dense, and yet the spirit is not in that vibration for very long, only for the length of time that it is housed within the physical body, that can be on times troublesome to one and all.

But you know, the seasons of your nature show you the rhythm of life, you know, and sometimes when you are feeling in despair of what life is about for you, then just listen to music; the rhythm of music can help you to raise your thoughts, to raise your awareness to the fact that life must continue after that point that you call death. Because otherwise, things would not make sense. And you all have, you know, very good minds when you are living in the physical body and you are having a physical life, because in that life, you see, you are learning and sometimes what you call coincidences pop up. But you know, there is no such thing, really, as a coincidence; it is just that you are unfolding in your own personal understanding and development of life.

For those very young here, you know, schoolwork can be arduous to say the least, but it is just stepping stones, you see, to prepare you for life, just as your family life prepares you to go out feeling secure into the world. How many of you think when I am grown up, I am going to do this; you have your heart set on certain things that you would wish to do with life, and sometimes it does not work out as you have imagined or as you have dreamt of. But you know, nothing in life means that you are failing, because it means you are taking on challenges, and from that, you know, you are evolving and learning. Because life is all about learning, whether you be young or old. Some of you may think that you keep repeating the same mistakes; there again, you know, nothing is the same, because you always have different challenges to face. But we want to tell you, you see, that it is important that you understand that life continues for that person that is part and parcel of your life, because sometimes, you know, you lose sight of the fact and think that, when the physical body is no more, then that person no longer exists. Which, you know, is something that is a little scary, and you know, even these sci-fi programmes have a lot of truth within them, but can be a little scary to watch.

It is important, you see, that you take things in your stride and take small steps forward. You would not be in school learning to read and be expected to be able to read a large encyclopaedia. You have to work your way through many things before you would have an understanding of the truth. And the thing is, you know, that perhaps you won't have a great understanding of the afterlife until you get there yourself. But you are all on the same journey, you see; you will all end up there because that is the natural rhythm of life. But if you know, without a shadow of doubt, that your loved ones are alive and well, then it makes it simpler. It makes you feel more buoyant, it makes you feel more settled within yourself. And loads of people have said, 'ahh, well, I think there's something after that point that we call death, but...' and it stops at the 'but'. But many other people are, what shall we say, investigators into things and take time out to realise that their own spirit is prompting them to understand the truth.

Communication does not take place just through a medium, you know, because you all have this mind, you all have this ability to think of somebody, and then they turn up, and you may not have seen them for quite some time, because we are all connected to one another through that vibration that we call love. Because you have a love for your fellow man, you have a love for your animals, you have a love of your nature, you have a love of life and the Creator of all life is God the Father. Not a gentleman that sits there and is going to judge you when you turn up in that world of light, but an energy that is the life force that runs through the whole of the universe. And even that very thought is quite scary to understand, because, when you live in a physical world, you like things in nice little pigeonholes, you know.

And you may have to face, through life, adversity; to understand the concept of life after death does not mean that you are excluded from life's lesson. In fact, you may have more to deal with, because you have a greater understanding of that spirit within you that sustains you whatever you face in life. It gives you strength, it gives you courage, it gives you hope, it gives you understanding, because it is life itself that you are encompassing, and so that is why it is important to take time out to remember your thoughts, to remember your dreams, because all things are possible when you look to moving forward and making yourself a better person. Because, you know, you should be thinking about how you treat yourself and how you treat others, so that you can begin to refine that spirit, that spirituality that is there within you. It says many things in the Bible, and one is an eye for an eye and a tooth for a tooth, but that seems a little bit barbaric, does it not? You know, you don't want to go out fighting one another; you want to find common ground on which you resonate with another. The common ground on which we all resonate is that of the spiritual essence of self. That is what keeps you motivated and keeps you moving forward and taking off the blinkers of superstition and of mistrust, and you know, you must open your mind and look at what things are of value to you. It is no good, we noticed, when we drove up, you know, our channel here noticed that your notice board has been vandalised, by a stone no doubt. But that was probably done by people that had nothing better to do, because they were bored out of their mind, because they were not using their creativity, and you know, if you give people something to think about and something to do, a goal to aim for, then you are going to get the very best out of that individual.

And that is what we ask of you: that you that you do your very best in life. To be treated as you would wish to be treated is a good yardstick, shall we say, because you are all in the same rhythm of living, but some, you know, they go off on a tangent and they become idealistic and not realistic, and then they are fighting for power over others. The idea is that we share in the power that comes from God the Father, the giver of all life.

And this is shown; as we said, the rhythm of life is shown in your seasons. You may have had a hard winter, but still the spring blossoms forth, followed by the summer and the autumn and the winter, and so the cycle continues endlessly. The cycle of life, my friends, continues endlessly, and you will meet up with those loved ones. You will meet up with those that you love, because it is the love tie that binds everything together.

And you know, if you went on holiday, you may be inclined, years ago, for the older people in the congregation to write a postcard to say 'wish you were here'. The youngsters may send a text, 'having a great time, wish you were here'. It is still communication, my friends, however you send the message, and so when our loved ones move on to the spirit world, they are excited about the idea that they may get a message back to you, in your dream state. In your mind's eye, you may be walking down a street and think that you are seeing that loved one that you have lost, and yet when you get closer up, it is just someone of the same stature, of the same build, of the same hair colouring, of the same shaped face, and then you are startled because it is not the person that you have lost that you can go up to. And that can be a little disconcerting, but it is, you see, a way of communication, because they use all of our senses to communicate with us.

Sometimes, you know, you may hear the same phrase going through your mind, and you may attribute that to something that your loved one used to say, when you were perhaps only a youngster, but all these memories are stored in our minds and can be utilised to give us that feeling that we are indeed in communication one with the other, because they would not go travelling on in their lives and not wish to communicate with us. That is a very simplistic way of telling you all about communication but, my friend, it does exist. It is not a figment of an overactive imagination. As we mentioned about coincidence, how this happened and that happened, and then your life suddenly became a lot better because you had met the love of your life, or you had met a dear friend, or you had met somebody that made a difference to you, because of their care, because of their love, because of their attention.

So we ask, my friends, that you do indeed give your

attention to the spirit world, that you make a promise to yourself that you will open your mind, and your heart, to their continued love, to know, without a shadow of a doubt, about their continued existence and yours also. Death is not a dead end. You know, in Port Talbot, our medium here gets lost up these little lanes, you know, and on her first visit, there was nothing happening with the sat nav, because it was confused with all the lanes, you see. And so you just go around in a circle when confusion reigns in your mind, so be decisive, be decisive with where you are going, what you are doing and what you want to understand about life. The more we learn, the more there is to learn. But remember that there is always a rhythm, a time to be born, a time to grow, a time to make your transition into the rebirth of new life. You have just celebrated Easter, which talks about life anew, talks about the fact that Jesus was taken out of the tomb and then ascended by the time Whitsun comes along, back to that spirit world, and in so doing, made many visitations to his family, to his friends, to those that he was teaching all about spiritual gifts, about the awareness that you have of the life beyond that of the matter.

So, enjoy your life is what we would say to you. When you feel that you are struggling and you are going nowhere, remember that your spirit is forever moving forward and learning and understanding about life as it unfolds for you as the individual. It is not all about the fact that we just say to you that your life will continue. You have those in the spirit world that will always be there close to you, trying to help you to understand this truth. Because, you know, there are those that suddenly make their transition into the spirit world, and you are left at a loss as to understand why that person had made their transition when they did, and why so suddenly.

There has been much in your news of those that have been killed en masse, whether it be through war or through these aeroplane disasters that have happened, and brought things very much into your mind's eye, of what has happened to these people when there is nothing left of their physical body. Their loved ones and their friends and those that are investigating what happened have many obstacles in their way before they see the light that they have not just died, but they have moved on in their life.

Difficult times, but it brings out much good within individuals when they are trying to come to terms with devastating news and devastating loss. It will always be so; we cannot make it easy, but you know, there is this understanding that life is a continuous process, and you are all going to move forward, and with what you call death, what we call rebirth, there is a newness of understanding and of how communication can be a two way process.

So, don't forget that you can talk to your loved ones in your mind, because that is how they communicate, mind to mind, on the vibration of the mind, and that is why it is good, sometimes, to sit in the silence of yourself. A little bit scary to begin with, but again the reading talked about the benefits of sitting quietly within your own mind, within your own self, and so give yourselves a pat on the back, my friends, for opening that mind, for coming into an establishment such as this, a little bit different, yes, but nevertheless you can see that it all begins to make sense when you start asking questions about the afterlife and more importantly about the rhythm of life.

Your universe, my friends, is a vast place, and there are many that research into all sorts of things, you know, but it has to make sense for you. One of you here could very well be another Einstein, but you know this has to make sense, we like to come forward to make sense to the ordinary person, so that you haven't got to be of an Einstein mentality to understand life.

And so, we say to you, my friends, go with the rhythm of life, enjoy the music of life, allow yourselves to go into that calm state from time to time, and know that you can always be around and about with those loved ones that walk this life with you to ensure that you do what is necessary and understand the truths of spiritual understanding. Be happy; that goes a long way, because sometimes sadness and loss can devastate you, but know that it is temporary when you know that that spirit within all of your loved ones and friends is something that will continue forever and ever, or for what we would term eternity.

And so, we leave this message of hope, of love, of understanding with you. It is important, you see, that you are just true to yourself. Because you know you better than anybody knows you, so be brave, be courageous and be good in what you are doing, be happy, and bring that love that you share with others, and use it wisely and then you cannot fail.

We say to you, my friends, good night and God bless.

Chapter Seven

Temple of Light Healing Sanctuary, Ystradgynlais, Swansea

SUNDAY 16TH MARCH 2008

GOOD EVENING to you (*Congregation: Good evening, White Feather, welcome*), my friends, that worship within this Temple of Light.

And as has been mentioned, you are entering into what you term Holy Week, when you should be thinking about the spirit, the spirit that you are. Because, you see, you are journeying through your life in the material world. God, the Great Spirit, as you understand it, sent to your world light of the spirit into human form, known as the Son of God. He had a journey to make and to fulfil the destiny of his individual spirit. And so, he worked with that spirit throughout his life, and took it upon himself to serve his spirit and his Father the Godhead. And all that sounds very, very grand, does it not? But you see, that life has been documented in your Holy Book, so you have many pages that you can read and read again, that will bring light to your spirit.

So, you are not walking in darkness or fear of the unknown. You are willing to express your spirit, the real you, because it is only your body that confines that spirit and that light. And so, you have to accept your limitations when your spirit is within the physical form, but you know that the spirit cannot die. And as the Lord made his journey into the city, having worked very hard in his ministry, showing to many how the spirit moves and how things are accomplished, that you can, indeed, change the course of another's life by allowing that spirit to fulfil its destiny. Because the spirit has to transform and rise out of the body and its confines, back to the realm of light. That is so for every spirit, whether that spirit is in animal form, whether it is in human form, or even from the mineral kingdom and that of nature. It will always transform itself, because that is what energy does. That's the laws of science.

And so, that should give you great joy. And then, when you have acknowledged the spirit, you realise that you have to walk forward in the light of the spirit. You cannot be afraid of what is in front of you when you are working with that spirit, and if in doubt then we tell to you to open that book; that will inspire you, uplift you in your darkness hour. For there are many in your world that suffer by way of physical or mental suffering, and sometimes spiritual suffering too. How do you think that Jesus felt when he realised his destiny? That he was going to allow his work to be known in as far and as many away places that he could find? He did not hide the gifts of the spirit, he worked with them, and he taught others also to work with the spirit so that the sick could be healed, so that those could be raised from the dead.

But then there were those doubters, those ones that were wishing him out of the way, because it was a threat to the very society in which they lived – but understanding his journey in life, and the purpose for that journey to bring that light of God into the world, so that it will shine within in all, forever and ever, making life easier once spiritual understanding has come about.

So, each one of you has work to do to understand your spirit. When faced with facing a rather horrendous death of the physical body, that man could have turned on his heels and run in the opposite direction. But he had a great faith and understanding of the power of the spirit, knowing that it had to be set free at some stage, to return back into the realm of light. That is the true story of Easter. Everybody was taught that the spirit would transcend back to those realms of light. He taught his disciples that very fact, but these truths, you know, did not always sit right, because there was a lack of understanding, perhaps a lack of dedication, perhaps a lack of courage. And yes, they wanted answers, because life was not easy in those days that you say are 2000 years ago.

And neither is life easy in your world today. There is so much that causes you to worry. There is so much fighting, so much illness, so much distrust in others. And so, the message that we would bring is that you trust in your spirit, in your true destiny, because you will move from one state of existence to another. Therefore, you will not die. You may not have understood that death is but the gateway to a new life, and Jesus understood this wholeheartedly, but he knew that he had to stand up to the opposition of the day.

And so it is that things do not change. You are all

standing up against those that would not understand this great truth, that would tell to you that you will die and that is the end, and so you will worry all of the time if that is so. We would tell you, the truth is that you will transform, your spirit will be set free, you will look and understand that you need to be using your spiritual gifts, that you need to be serving others, because you are all interdependent upon one another. Jesus was to a certain extent dependent upon his disciples, because the work that they did reflected on how he taught them.

And so it is that those teachings continue, even today, and there are many that strive to bring that power of the spirit to the forefront of their lives, and in so doing help all those that are struggling in their life, struggling with a failing physical body, struggling with a failing mind. Because you all have strong minds, do you not, that sometimes keep you in the darkness and away from the light, and so you have to be brave and courageous; that is why we would ask you not just to think about the journey of your life in this one week when it culminates in the resurrection of the spirit.

You see, you cannot ever leave those that you love, because it is the tie of love that binds all together. When you make your transition into the world of light, you will be allowed to come back into the confines of the physical world, and those that are open minded will be able to feel your presence, to pick your thoughts of love, and so it is that the Christ light will walk with you, but you have to attune yourself to that very power otherwise you may be going down the wrong pathway of life. Thinking that you are all powerful, that you are all loving, your spirit truly is, but if you can allow yourself to link with the essence of God and the light of Jesus, because he still very much wants you to aspire to those teachings that he brought, not just for twelve disciples to carry on his work, but for every one of you to carry on the work of the spirit, to be true to that spirit and know that you cannot fail. When you understand that you have these gifts and this divine spark within you, then you know that you are on this journey that will never, ever end. However you face the death of your physical body will not matter. It does not matter that it has to be quick, or whether it is slow; it means that your spirit will continue its journey, and that is why it is so important to remember the Easter time because life is anew.

When you have awakened the spirit within you, there is no going back to the darkness, to the uncertainty of life; you are certain you know that the power can change not only you and your life, and your understanding of it, but you too, by being of service, can inspire and uplift others that are perhaps not quite as illumined as yourself. That is why we would tell to you to stay within the light, not to stray from the light. Because there are temptations out in your world that can perhaps turn you away from your true self. Understand who you are, what you are. You are spirit, you cannot fail in your life, but sometimes you may feel that life has failed you.

Just as Jesus had the crowd on his side as he made his entry into the city of Jerusalem. They were all praising the name of the Lord, the King, the Messiah that had been long awaited, and then things took, as you may say, a turn for the worse, and within five days, that same man, that same human being was put to death, or at least, his physical body returned to the earth. The spirit left, but he had to fulfil the prophesy and the journey of his spirit. And so he showed himself, on that Easter day, to those that were mourning the loss of his life. Was his life lost? Certainly not; it had been transformed. Again, if you go a bit further along, it gets into the realms of understanding the spirit and the power of it, because at Whitsun time, then the spirit ascended back into the realms of light. The spirit cannot be broken, it cannot die.

That is the whole of the ministry of the Christ. The Christ light, you call it; take it, it is yours to see. Do not let it blind you, because you can be blinded by the light, but once that has happened then you can begin to feel comfortable and understand spirituality, spiritual things are forever.

You cannot turn away from that destiny, and that is why you are celebrating the death, a very gruesome death, on that cross. But look what has been accomplished as a result, by one individual, that was only doing his Father's work. You are all workers, my friends, that is good, yes? You can get busy then, and do all the work that you must to bring that light into your world that has much desire to be helped.

So do not shirk. We only ask to work in the light, then you cannot fail. If you have any doubts, then look into your book and see all those encounters that happened showing the ministry of the spirit. You administer through your spirit and allow your mind to be flooded by the light, and transformation will follow within your world. Never ever give up hope. Because life after death, of the physical body, is assured. 'Blessed Assurance, Jesus is Mine' that is all that we have to say.

Follow the light, use the light. Be happy in the light and you will see the glory of your work. Because you are working daily to your spiritual home where you can return at any time that your spirit so desires. Because that is the only sure thing about life, is that you are going to die. That is not quite as difficult as it sounds. The fear of death is very difficult for many to face; because of the love that you have for one another, you feel comforted when the physical presence is still with you. But rest assured that you get a greater comfort knowing that the spiritual essence of your loved ones are always there for you, to support you, to guide you and to bring out of you that love, that spiritual love. Because it is the spirit that is immortal. It may be intangible, you cannot see it, but it is the power that drives you forward, that gives you courage, that gives you strength to face all things that you consider to be adverse. So, we bring that light, we leave that light, and we rejoice in the love that you share within this Temple of Light and say to you, my friends, good night and God bless.

EASTER SUNDAY 23RD MARCH 2008

GOOD EVENING to you, my friends. *(Congregation: Good evening.)*

Thank you. It's a pleasure to come and to talk with you. Do you realise that you have created the vibration within this temple that allows ease of delivery? Because we enjoy the journey back to this sanctuary, because you know, your earth is very dense. There is not much light that shines forth, and the more that you link with your spirit and those in the spirit world, the stronger your light becomes. And so that ease of entry is helped. You have seen, from time to time, these rockets that leave your earth for space, and have to break through the earth's atmosphere into that vastness of space. And sometimes it is perhaps a little difficult to comprehend how all that happens. And yet, when you send your thoughts out for help to God, imagine that you are letting off a rocket into space, but it is a guided missile, you know, to the source of all life. And so it is that that spirit within you, at the point of physical death, will have a rebirth into the realm of spirit, of light, the eternal light that will forever shine, so that upon your earth, ignorance and fear is banished and no more.

Easter time is one of great joy for us in the spirit world, because it focuses attention that you cannot die. That the spirit will be reborn back to the source, to the Creator that you call God. The story has unfolded through Holy Week, has it not? Symbolising the journey, a journey that you all make of the spirit, so that you come to the realisation that you will indeed face that rebirth, back into the light.

It is very important, you see, that you share your

knowledge and understanding with others that are fearful of life in total. Fearful of their life on the earth and even more fearful of their life that will continue in the spirit realms. That saddens us, and that is why we will always bring you joy. For you are all seeking understanding, and that is good. That is why the light within this sanctuary is always burning brightly, and do you know that we bring souls here to observe the work that you do? Because they need healing also, and sometimes they are nearer your earth vibration than they are to our vibration within the spirit realms. What shall we call it, 'halfway house'? Because, you see, it is important that you work with your own spirit, so that your transition will be complete.

And when Mary was outside of that tomb, there was no body lying inside. Because the transition into the spirit world had begun. And so, when Jesus spoke to her, she was unaware of who that person was. In disguise, you may say. Perhaps she thought he was the gardener that tended to the earth. And, indeed, Jesus was the gardener, who was tending to the souls of mankind. He came with a message to give, knowledge to impart, so that he taught those that were willing to listen, and they did not fully understand the message, because life was certainly not going to end at the point that you call death.

And so, he was still working upon his mission, and so it is in your world also. You are working on your mission, and how many of you have had experiences of understanding that your loved ones are indeed with you, although their physical body is no more. You have had your own communication with the spirit world, your own communion with those that you love. This is what working with the spirit is all about. Death cannot sever the bonds of love.

That is why we endeavour, from time to time, to talk with you, to give that understanding that there is this power and this energy that allows us to focus and come into the earth's vibration once again. And Jesus said that it was only temporary, because he had not fully transcended back to the spirit realm; he was betwixt and between, perhaps is a good phrase to use. Because we can, you see, stand at different levels of vibration to aid our communication, and so he had to get the message across to his students to tell them, wake up, see the light, see that I am around and about, become aware of my presence. It is all good sci-fi stuff, is it not? You believe all that, but do you believe, truly believe, that you are spirit here and now?

You are travelling, you are journeying forward with that light. How do you build that bridge between the two worlds? Well, Jesus taught his disciples exactly how to link with the spirit within, and indeed the spirit without. They were always coming together to share in their experiences, just as you would share within your own circles of learning and understanding. Because you study these things, you study how you work with the spirit world, a natural ability within all of you that has to be nurtured.

There are many in your world, you know, that do not understand the Easter message. They are not sure whether you are celebrating the birth of Jesus or the death of Jesus; they did a survey only this week for the media, and many thought it was a time only for children to eat eggs! How sad is that? Yes, okay, the egg is symbolic of new life. Your springtime is symbolic of new life. The spirit is going always forward into different realms of understanding and of light. So be joyous that you have built upon the vibration of the spirit, that there is this energy that moves, has life, can show you the power of the spirit in action. You have to be of service, you see. Give of yourself. Be brave and know that you are about God's work. That is the important issue.

The spirit is going to rise, you know; resurrection is new life. And to rise up means that you are moving forward. Yes, the 'R' will stand for resurrection that means that you are going to move forward. The 'I' could be inspiration; perhaps we should consider it to be intelligence, because there is this great intelligence that is the power that is leading forward to dispel darkness in your world. Too many are busy sending their rockets into space, not many are busy understanding their own spirit, that is going to be sent into that realm of spirit when you are no more a physical being. 'S' perhaps could be that of service, because many of us come forward to tell you that it is only that we seek to serve, so that you can endeavour to be a servant of God. Jesus served supper to his disciples, yes, maybe called followers but really they were not; they were going to become pioneers to continue the work of the spirit. And yes, they were bereft that their leader was no more, or so they thought, forgetting all about the prophesy that the spirit was going to rise, that there was going to be a resurrection, that the life would continue in that new vibration of light and love. A vibration that we work on all of the time. We are busy running and up a down a ladder, you may say, because we have to work, as best as we can, to bring the truth forward, and you see the 'E' out of that word 'rise' will signify that you have an eternity to fulfil your work. No limitations there then; you cannot say that you are too old. Age is nothing, just a number. Perhaps you would disagree, because the poor body, you know, it goes through stages all of its own, and can become a little nuisance from time to time. But even in the weakest of bodies the spirit can be strong.

That is why we bring you back to this joyous time of Easter. No end, only beginnings anew. That information should be shouted from the rooftops. The power of the spirit brings healing for all. All that is asked, that you open your hearts and minds to all those spiritual things that are written about, in your books, that the Masters, many of them, have come to tell you, come to show you as well, and in that doing and in that work you can join in. It did not stop all those years ago; it just began to filter through humankind to get them focused on that love.

The true message of Easter, my friends, is to dispel your fear of the unknown, to tell to you that you have everlasting life. What sort of legacy is that? You have to be joyous, you have to worship that great Creator, God. You come into the world understanding your spirit, you will go out of the physical world understanding your spirit. But in those intervening years, of your earth world you will have learnt a great deal if you work with your spirit. And we cannot thank you enough for the service that you give. No reward, perhaps only more difficulties from day to day. But you have that wonderful power of prayer that will always sustain you.

Mary was outside of that tomb, praying for her Lord. He answered the call, he showed himself to her. But it wasn't until he spoke that she realised who was bringing that message, because the physical appearance was not obvious to her; so you see, many angels and guides and helpers can very often come in disguise. It may be your next-door neighbour, it may be your friend, it may be a passer-by in the street.

You are all servants of God working with your spirit. Take the help that is given, take the knowledge that is imparted, and walk tall with your spirit because it is shining the light. It is calling all those that need help just to walk in your path, so that you can fulfil your work whilst on earth, your spiritual work. It is a journey on which you cannot fail.

The journey into Jerusalem lead to the death of the physical body because the masses did not understand. Jesus was, to use a modern phrase, a target, a threat to the authorities who wanted power. So, they thought, well this is easy, we rid ourselves of the physical presence of that person and that will be that. Hmm, I do not think so. Because the spirit moves on and there are no boundaries; the spirit always manifest itself whenever and wherever it can, to be of service to those that are in need.

That is why you have this wonderful sanctuary of light, so we give our thanks for the work that you do, not only within these four walls but within the community, within the far distant shores, because there are links all over your earth world, and we in the spirit world are always excited when the spirit expands and the work carries on. There is no end to life. Take that as a truth. Banish your fear. The message of Easter: we bring joy, we bring love and those two things bring you, the individual, peace. A peace which passes all understanding. Take your knowledge, do your work, and the work of the spirit will continue unhindered, forever and ever.

We say, to you, good night and God bless.

SUNDAY 3RD MARCH 2013

GOOD EVENING to you, my friends, *(Congregation: Good evening, White Feather),* it is a pleasure to come and to talk with you.

And it is tangible, the silence that you created waiting for the voice. And that is good, you know, because you are respectful of the spiritual energies that are here within this Temple of Light, and so we are able to use that energy when we can channel those from the spirit world that would wish to come and to speak with you. Because, you know, you all have questions do you not, about your own spirituality, about your own spiritual awareness.

You read many things that you ponder over and ask questions about, and the reading this evening was telling to you the miracle of feeding of the five thousand, and you know when our channel came in this evening, she sat in the kitchen and what was spoken about was the food banks that are springing up all over your country, because people have seen the need, because of the times in which you live. Austerity they call it, and everyone is supposed to be not able to function quite as well in the material world and so you see the spirit within many individuals is working well within your communities, because you do not have to follow any religion, at all, for your spirit to be prompted to aid others that you consider to be less fortunate then yourselves.

You see, when Jesus walked the earth, many followed him because they were wanting to understand about spirituality and spiritual enlightenment, and so there were many that would walk and follow him, and during the time of his preaching and channelling of the

191

spirit there were times when people needed indeed to be fed, for the physical body is in need all of the time of sustenance, and not only the spiritual part of you.

And so, he took it upon himself to ensure that food was given in abundance and everybody there shared the same food, and yet when they had finished eating and were full, there was still enough and more that was gathered that would be able to be used at another time. And so, you see, in your world there are those that are enlightened from their spirit within, and as you sit here in this environment, you have all used your mind to project outwards healing, and that enables us in the spirit world to use that energy and that vibration, to take it to wherever it is needed, so that nobody is left in darkness, for everyone that walks your material world, in the physical body, is aided by the spiritual realms and their own spirit within, and you are all journeying together, and so it is that you will be pulled by your own spirit to help those that are less fortunate than yourselves, to feed them spiritually as well as physically.

There has been much to worry you in the producing of food, within your country alone, for there have been floods, there have been many things that have been brought to light. People cutting corners, you may think, and contaminating your food chain. But you know, you need to keep things simple; you need to be able to understand nature itself, for there is enough food for one and all if it is shared one with the other. We put too many labels on things, you know, that this is yours and that is theirs; the same too with your spiritual gifts; you have them from the spirit world in abundance. And the same as you need food to keep your body going, we would ask you that you share your spiritual attributes also to give people that shining light that you are, so that they can follow your example. You need to come into a sanctuary such as this to spend a little time in that silence of your own self, of your own soul, so that you can use your spirituality in your day to day living, sharing with one and all. It is important, you see, that you take on board all that is shown to you.

Through eons of time, and in your Holy Book, the work of the spirit is unconditional. You all benefit from that power that you call God, that we call Love. And so, it is important that you understand that the spirit needs to be nourished and replenished, just as the body does also. We ask that you gather together at certain times so that the light becomes brighter, that it is sent out into the ether to be used for the greater good of mankind. It all looks doom and gloom in your world, yes, but you must remember that the world is evolving.

Day to day miracles happen where you can't find logical explanation, but you see it is the power of the spirit moving amongst you, moving around you, and you may suffer daily from your viruses and goodness knows what, but the body is the temple for the spirit. And you will overcome all ailments of the body, that is part and parcel, for the spirit is unaffected and the spirit will move on in time back to the world of light. Back to our realms of Love and harmony, and so we do not want you to waste time worrying about incidentals, because, you see, the world has to unite in peace and love, all spiritual attributes that are sometimes forgotten, and so we ask you just to remember to send your thoughts to be the spirit world, because all things are possible. The love that passes all understanding is God's love, the Creator of all, and that should be open in your minds to realise that nothing is open to debate, all things need to be shared one with the other, and then miracles occur, all of the time. Too many are indeed in darkness of fear.

But it is your work within your world to dispel that fear, take the fear from own mind and know that, in so doing, you can inspire others, you can all feed the world. In fact, there was, many years ago, a song that included those words that was to do with famine in a certain part of the world, and great work was done, and so it is from time to time you will see that the world does indeed respond to the needs of the humans that inhabit that material plane. And so, don't lose hope, just do your work, use your spiritual attributes wisely, and things will begin to take a turn for the better. Do not become enmeshed in materialism; look to the light for your inspiration. Use your inspiration and your endeavours will indeed work wonders.

There should be no one in your world that suffers, but within your world many lessons have to be learnt. There are those that are materially endowed and those that aren't. But it is all about sharing, it is all about the spirit responding to those that are in need on many, many different levels, so that is why we give you the hope, that we bring you the love, that we bring you the contentment, that we bring you the peace of mind for all the things that you read about, from those that walked eons of time ago, showing the power of the spirit can be taken up by yourselves so that you can make a difference, for that is what you are here, on the earth, to do.

So do not think that it is impossible; take up the challenge, revive yourself by coming into this temple where the spirit works tirelessly for the best to be accomplished within your community, within your world. Take that peace, take that love, for your spirit will move forward, your understanding will become clearer, and you will realise that the spirit that is within you is an eternal being, and you are progressing all of the time towards the light, towards the perfection, of God the Creator.

And so, we say to you, my friends, good night and God bless.

SUNDAY 6TH OCTOBER 2013

GOOD EVENING to you, *(Congregation: Good evening White Feather)* my friends, it is a pleasure to come and to talk with you, and you certainly do manage, all of the time, to provide a reading that is contentious.

Because there are many different views that can be taken on that passage that was read about the healing ministry of Jesus, and how difficult it was, and we know too, that this Temple of Light is primarily a healing sanctuary, because you are on a healing mission, you see, and that is good. Because the physical body will always be troublesome to the individual at some time or another, because the physical body is but a temple for the spirit. And that temple has to one day be left by the spirit, for the spirit to continue its journey of life. But at that point, when the spirit leaves the body, you call it death, we call it life anew, for the spirit, you see. And so, there will always be the sickness of the body, of the mind, but never sickness of the spirit, so that is what we have to say to you to make things a little bit clearer.

And sometimes, you see, when Christ was doing his ministry of healing, he would choose those that had physical problems because it showed up the power of the spirit and the power of the healing vibration of love. Because, you see, people would take notice, because they could see it with their physical eyes, that the man with palsy would then be able to have mobility. And so, you see, all these things, when you are not spiritually enlightened, you need these signposts given to you in a very fundamental way, so that you cannot put it down to coincidence or to luck or to anything else, that somebody waved a magic wand; it was part of that soul's journey to have the physical affliction lifted away at that time, for that man with palsy was also spirituality enlightened you see.

And some of those in your world that are afflicted physically, they are the strong beacons of light, in your world, that then facilitate those of you that channel the power of the spirit to do the work that you are able to do because of your own spirituality. And so, you see, it is quite a complex situation, is it not? But what you need to know is that all of the time people are alleviated of their suffering in ways that may be unseen to you, but is known to us in the spiritual realms of light. And so, we want you to be full of hope, we want you to know that healing only brings benefit, and that indeed is the true light of Christ that shines in your world.

You have to have darkness to appreciate the light; you have warmth, which you have a lot of, to appreciate cold, which you have a lot of, you see, just in this one year of your calendar; so you may say that it is extremes, and so it is that sometimes the most extreme case of sickness is the one that will pull through and make a physical recovery, you see, just to show to others the power of the spirit.

In your world you have made many strides forward in your world of medicine and medical technology, but still not everyone can be cured and their physical body be well once more, but there are many that do, because it is part of their karma to go through many different challenges in life. And so we don't want you to look at somebody who is ill as the poor one; it just means that their spirit is evolving towards the new world of the spirit, you see, because you have to grow and flourish and move on.

Many people are directed to come in through these doors for help, and many I am sure come in and go out and do not return, for reasons best known unto themselves, but rest assured that they have been helped, you see. And sometimes, as individuals you turn yourself away from the help that is offered, because that too is part of your karmic journey through life.

So, all you have to remember is that you have to be true to yourselves, each one of you, and take on the responsibility of your own spirituality, of your own spiritual understanding. Jesus not only brought forward acts of healing, but he taught those that worked with him, his chosen ones, to do exactly the same as he, and so that means that you all have the ability to work with your own spirit and use your own gifts to be able to help others, to give them a little bit of encouragement when they feel that they are in darkness, that they are fearful of the outcome of their illness, of their challenge, of their problems in life.

And so, we are all capable of channelling the spirit, and those in the spirit world are only too willing to help us along the way. Christ never took on to himself the worries and the problems of others, because he was always prayerful, and so he would send out to those in the spirit world and to the great Creator that you call God for assistance, in all the work that he did; and so it is that that is the way forward in life, to bring that great power of love to the confines of the earth, into the arena, for all those that are willing to open their hearts and minds to the understanding that the spirit within allows them a life of eternity. And so there is no end, only new beginnings, and as complex as that reading was, it brings forward enlightenment for you to know that you can, indeed, face all adversity and still know that you are going to journey forward in life.

It is very difficult to leave behind what you know as reality. It is very difficult to leave behind the family that you love, the friends that are dear to you, and all that connect to you, but you know, the time will come when we all have to say goodbye to the physical connection to the earth, and to the others that we connect to through that love tie, for each one of us has a purpose and a journey to fulfil, to bring forward that light, to share in that light, and to share in the love of God the Father. Jesus walked the earth to demonstrate the power of the spirit, in many and varied aspects. Healing was one of those aspects of spiritual understanding and enlightenment. So, take up the challenge, my friends. Take out the message that you know to be true, that your life will continue whatever you have faced in the physical form. It is but a transition to the next realm of existence.

And you know, when many suffer physical problems, it helps your medical profession to adapt and reform and understand and push the boundaries out for more and more help to be given to those that suffer, they are marching forward all of the time. But you know, there are many that have short spans of life in the physical world, and others that have longer lives, but you know, it does not matter whether it is short, medium, or long, and we are not talking about your clothes, we are talking about the idea that you have to move forward at the time that is right for your own spiritual growth, and that is all that matters.

So, do not look upon those that suffer physically in a way that you feel sorry for them, because they sometimes are truly enlightened from their own spirit, and that makes their life quite adaptable, you see, and they can soon realise when they return to the spirit realms the work that they have done has been good, to make others sit up and take notice because they are a little different from others because of the problems and the adversity that they face as an individual but that moulds the personality that they are in the physical body; and it moulds the spirit that they truly are, to shine that light further and further forward to bring in those that are fearful of the unknown and not willing to unfold their own spiritual gifts and their own spirituality.

I hope that that has brought some to that greater understanding of what illness and sickness is about in your world. So, know that no one suffers, as you would see, endless pain unless they keep themselves in the darkness, away from the light of the truth, and then their life can be very difficult, but all of the time they are assisted by those that walk with them, and so it is that we have to intermingle the one world with the other, the physical with the spiritual, and in so doing you are about God's work.

And so you are taking up your own ministry and basing it on the life and the works of many of the avatars that came before, in eons of time gone by, but you know, you need to have that understanding of the true essence of the spirit of God the Father. So read these words, in these books, and take on board the message that is there for each one of you according to your need, so you always remember that the doors of a sanctuary, such as this, are always open, and encourage others to come through those doors to seek answers to questions and fears that they may be carrying with them needlessly. For the truth is the truth, the light is the light; we want to banish all darkness within your world, then peace would indeed come to your earth. There would be changes beyond your comprehension, but we work tirelessly to use anyone that is willing to take on board the truth that there is no death, but life is truly eternal.

And so, we say to you, my friends, good night and God bless.

GOOD EVENING to you, my friends, *(Congregation: Good evening White Feather, welcome)* it is a pleasure to come and to talk with you.

It is very difficult, at times, is it not, to understand the workings of the spirit? Of the spirit within you, the individual, and of the spirit within those that you may not know. For you know, it is always with sadness that we have to talk with you about hostilities between those of the human race. It brings sadness to you as you listen to all those conflicts that are apparent within your physical world. And yet you have heard, at the beginning of this service, of what you would term a miracle, when one individual was not hurt in any way, in the physical form. And so, you see, we can protect, we can help, and your prayers and thoughts are living things that aid and abet us, in our work, from the spirit world realms of life.

Because, you know, when you pray you want everything in the physical world to be at peace, and that is more than admirable, and your reading talked about taking up arms, and fighting for what you believe in and what you know to be right, for one and all. But how do you convince others about peace? when they, within themselves, have a hidden agenda that cannot be seen, and as was said, they were taken into the fold of a spiritual establishment, within your physical world, and yet their views, the knowledge that they had gained; and that will mean that when they progress and move back to the realms of light, then they have to make amends. And so you see it is you, the individual, that has to forgive you, the individual, for your actions whilst you are in the physical form of life. And that is why, you see, you have to look beyond the confines of matter. And that is very difficult, you see. That is why, from time to time, we send to you those that have led by the light of the spirit, that can perform what you term miracles, because it is that individual's pathway to prove to the sceptic, to those that only want to fight for what they think is right, for power, for the individual.

And so, we have to dispel some of the things that happen in your world, dispel the fear from your minds and your hearts when you are looking towards the spirit for help and direction. And so, it is good to use the negative state for you to link with your own true self, and for the power of the spirit world to come in, for your benefit, you the individual; that is what is important. There are many that come to lead a spiritual existence, to shine their light, and you know they are subject to oppression, to ridicule and goodness knows what by other humankind that cannot see what life is truly about, because you should be able to share one with the other, and yet under the auspices of oppression and conflict, the power of the spirit it can be seen to be working for the best, for many. And so you might think that those carrying the banner forward for the light are being held back in some way, and not making progress, and yet progress is being made.

All of the time the planets of the universe change their alignment, one to the other, and this has an effect on your earth also, and so you are moving towards, you see, the Aquarian age, you are in it, and things have to change and things will change, and they will change for the better in time. But it cannot be seen because everybody is struggling for power for themselves, and not for the benefit of everything and everyone. And so, through eons of time, we have explained that it is not that you should be fighting one another, or even yourself; you should be accepting of the power of the spirit.

Within your world there are many that are grief stricken at the loss of loved ones and friends, and this is part of being a human individual when the spirit is encased by that physical form, and that physical form and that physical mind is wanting to be in control. And sometimes, you know, taking control, it makes your world become out of control. And this is mainly the problem. Whoever enters into a spiritual environment and does not understand the spirit within themselves then, as you have witnessed, the things go awry, and the last person, or people, that you would expect to cause harm, then they come forward and do what seems to be wicked work in your world.

But you know, there are too many that we would consider are brainwashed into thinking that they have to become martyrs to bring power to too many in your world. Your world has to turn itself, on its head, to use modern terminology, because, you see, it is progressing forward, and the individual will not have power over the individual when the motives behind that power are not in alignment with the God energy of life. And so too, much harm cannot be done, and that is why that story was told to you about that lady that was walking in danger, but was not physically hurt.

The problem being, of course, that as a sensitive, that individual will take some time to feel comfortable again in the work that she and the unit, together, are doing. And yet she now has a lifeline to this Temple of Light, which we talk to you about every time we come forward, because people are drawn in, whether it is via you, and many use technology by way of email. We have a batch of technology in our world, because it is spirit to spirit, not computer to computer or handheld phone. We have better ways of working it out, because our batteries do not fail, you see. If your batteries do wear themselves out, then communication easily stops, and you have to find a power source to plug back in; so we are light years ahead of your technology, you see. And that is good, because that shows to you how the power of God is indestructible, and will never cease to communicate to you earthlings. Because you are only firing on one cylinder, and that is usually of the material, when we fire on all cylinders that are spiritual.

And so that should bring back to you hope and, what shall we say, confidence, because that is what happened this evening on hearing that sad news: all your confidence disappeared. But you know, you have to be confident about the spirit that is within you, that motivates you to go forward, but allows you time to send out your thoughts, your living thoughts, that, as we said, we use.

In your Holy Book, the Bible, we talk about war all of the time, because it has never stopped happening in your world that one sect will fight another because they have different ideas, but they are forgetting about the truth of the spirit. And so, you should all be linking with each other, and that is what happens when you work on a spiritual level. Of course we do not need batteries to power that spiritual activity, we need you, the human being that is the spirit and part of God the Creator. If you can feel peace within yourself, then that is what we need, because when you do that you are not going to fight with other people, whether it be family or friends, because you will be spiritually alive, and then when that goes out to other individuals, when they get to that place of peace within themselves, then your world will start to calm down and be less, what shall we say, volatile. Because, you know, you only have to strike a match in wrong place, the wrong circumstances, and a fire will erupt. If the other things are all equal your world seems to be in turmoil, but we will say to you that it is only change happening all at once, and eventually there will be a breakthrough that will please those in the spirit world. Because there are many that are truly enlightened by the spirit, and as much as they invite other people to work with the spirit, if they are not worthy to be true to themselves and their own spirit, then you are going to get more volatility in your world and not calmness and peace.

So, saying it in that way, you and we have a lot of work to do. But, as we said, all avenues of communication are open and not reliant upon battery power that fails. Reliant on power that is within you, the power of the spirit, so that is why we need you as an army, not to take up arms, but to take up the spirit and to fight for what you know is the truth. And the truth is that you are only encased within that physical body, and if it was, what shall we say, problematic to the individual, eventually that body will not be needed as a vehicle for the spirit, because the spirit always transcends what you term to be death. So even when all these people are wiped off your earth through war and conflict, they are alive and well in our world and ready to fight for the right cause. That of peace, you see. So, that will tell to you that you, the individual, are your own worst enemy for misunderstanding power of the spirit and the truth. And so that seems a little harsh, we know, but you will see when you find, when you find harmony and accept the love of God the Creator, then your world will begin to show signs of coming back to spiritual life. And, you know, as you enter springtime, your world, is springing into life, in the form of nature. The spirit world springs into life with you, the individual, and there are many that do understand how to work with those energies from God the Father.

And so, we don't bring you despair, we bring you hope, but more importantly we bring you peace. But we want you to feel that things are moving forward and that spirit within you is being ignited, yet again, as you begin a new season and you see life coming back into nature. Because your world also works in cycles, you see, and yes, if something is not newsworthy, because it has been running a long course, it does not mean that there is not a need, and that is why you are linked in to that particular country, but you from that, are going to see how the spirit takes charge. Not control, because we cannot control your world. You have to do that. But when it is controlled by the spirit of mankind, then things will begin to change, so that it can be seen how the forces of light work. Illumination comes to the individual that is prepared to give time to themselves and their true self, that of the spirit.

So you see, that reading ended with that prayer that you are all familiar with, a prayer to the Father God, and that prayer may be considered by some to be imagined, because it can be said quite quickly, without you understanding the power behind the words. And yet what it does, a mantra and that type of prayer, immediately puts your mind into the spiritual mode of life and gives it the energy to be able to be used for the best by those ambassadors of light that work close to your earth plane, and so that it can be reinforced in our world to give it more energy. To give it more battery power, you see. To kick us into action. To define the spot where the action is needed the most. You know, really the power of the spirit is needed everywhere, in your world, because too many people abuse the power of the spirit, because they only work on the material vibration of themselves and life. And that is when you take from the earth plane, but they do not give back, and then, of course, it looks as though devastation is what is in order. But we tell you not to worry, because the spirit will always transcend that of the material, you see, and it is why that lady was unharmed as the result of destruction there in the physical world. And so we want you to take this forward, and perhaps, yes, to take up arms, but not with guns and all those weapons that are used in warfare, but to take up arms with the very power that is you, the spiritual self, you see. And then you will begin to see the light goes forth and shines in the darkest corner of your earthly world. So, remember these links that you are making, to various parts , because there is much that can be gained from a true association of spirit to spirit. And do not despair about those that come into a spiritual place and use the power in an unwise way. Because they too are helped to see the light, but of course, until they see the light they can cause a great deal of devastation, but they cannot win, and so your world of matter is safe, just a little bit difficult to live within. It is good that we are able to talk to you directly. It is good that you listen. It is good that you act upon what you know to be right. It is good that you take time to worship the spirit, because they do help us to see how it is that we can move those spiritually enlightened forward in their lives. So do not despair; be happy, and do your work, as you said, maybe in secret, it does not matter, because you know sometimes when you are in that power of the spirit then we can utilise those thoughts and that energy to help us to spread out and to be a beacon and to help those that are ready to listen and work in that light, in that love. So do not despair of those that seem to lose their way, because they have to make amends. It is not anybody else's problem, but those individuals that are a little bit mixed up, within their own hearts and minds and within their own spirit also.

So, we work unceasingly with your thoughts, with your spirit, to maintain that communication between God the Father and those beings in your world that are there to bring that work forward, and that light, so that your world is kept safe and well.

And so, we say to you, my friends, good night and God bless.

GOOD EVENING to you, my friends, *(Good evening, White Feather and welcome)* it is a pleasure to come and to talk with you.

And to instil within you that knowledge and understanding that you are spirit, you are part of the Father God, because it important that you understand your spiritual pathway in life. For each one of you has that pathway that is for you and only you.

In that reading, we heard how John was there doing his work, linking with his spirit within and with God the Father, to bring people to the understanding that they should be baptised in the river, as a testimony to their way of life, as they too, walk forward to bring the light of Christ into the world and allow it to have expression. You see, whilst you walk your pathway, you will be asked, well, who are you, and what are you doing, what right do you have to give a testimony to your understanding of the spiritual realms of life?

And so, it was John that baptised Jesus, for he too was on a spiritual pathway, but although they were related in family, they had different pathways to follow to expand their spirituality and their spiritual awareness. And they were both to be questioned throughout their lives on their purpose, because the authorities in those days were asking many questions, because they already had power over most of the land, shall we put it that way. And so, you see, you will always be up against authority, authority within your material, physical world, those that think they know the answers to all of the problems, whereas in point of fact they are making more problems, and they do not realise what they are

210

doing. In your world, there is much that causes concern to us in the spirit world.

There is much that causes concern to you as a community, as an individual, but you must have faith in the power of the spirit. For those in the spiritual realms of light always band together, so that there are those that we can use as channels; just as Christ was a channel for us in the spirit world, you too can be a channel to shine that light for good and healing. You have done so in this service, up to now, for you have given time to think of all those in need. You have given time to think of your own needs, and of those that you know that are in need that would wish to have help from the higher realms of life.

And so, you see, that is all good, because we are able then to use that light in its abundance, for the more that you open out your own spirituality, the brighter the light that is carried forward to our world. And so, yes, you have links in many far-reaching places in your world, and we have links also within your world, because it is a constant duty of ours, as those enlightened ones from the realms above, to keep guard on what is happening in your world.

Because, you see, there is much worry and trouble, there is much negativity in your world, because of people wanting power; and you see, misuse of power does not help, it just causes a lot of panic within individuals, and when a life is lost in your world it must be remembered that it is a rebirth in our world. And so there is no harm to the individual spirit, it is only harm to the physical body that was housing that spirit, that individual, that soul that will move on and try to link in with all those that wish to give aid and understanding about spirituality, about the spirit light, about the world that is thought, that has nothing to do with the physical existence.

There are so many in your world that are disinterested in understanding about a spiritual life, a spiritual life that you live here and now. Not a spiritual life that you just live when you return to those realms of the spirit world minus your physical body. That is why there is so much written about Christ's ministry along the earth plane; but he was always put to the test, he was always asked difficult questions, he was always put out into what you may term the firing line.

And today in your world, it is not religion that is important; it is the motive with which you use your spirituality and your gifts. Because they can indeed move mountains, you see. Too many wish to wear labels and say they are this, they are that or the other, and then they are fighting for recognition, and that is how your wars start, because they want to oppress the spirit within mankind, and we want to ignite the spirit within mankind to bring forward that light, that peace, that you all yearn for. It is a little tough to live in the physical world, to live with your spirit confined within the physical body, but you are all present in the physical in order to shine the light, forward, of the spirit.

And so, that is the crux of the matter, that is why the authorities will always want to know what you are about, what you are doing, and be amazed at the work that can be accomplished through a strong connection with the realms of light. Because you have always, from this particular environment, managed to push that light forward into various corners of your world, of your earth world, and we aid at every opportunity that we can.

And so, we want you to understand that you can play your part, you can indeed have that courage, have that faith, have that trust; look within the Holy book to find many answers, because, as we say, Christ was always being questioned and having to give forth answers that were understood by the individual but by the masses also. He brought peace, he brought love in abundance, but even his efforts were, what shall we say, not appreciated by the powers that were there in that day, that wanted to rule over everybody, you see. And they thought the way to win through, of course, was to crucify that one individual, and yet you know the story didn't end at that point that you call death, because it was only the death of the physical body. And that is for everyone; whoever you are, what you are doing is what is important, so take up your arms, my friends, not in the way of guns, and treachery such as that, but in the power that you own, that is the spirit within you.

Because in so doing, then there will be much in your world that will change, that will change for the better. And the first thing that we ask of you is that you find peace within your own mind, within your own self, as you go through your day to day living. Because it is in the day to day living that you have to forge forward, because there are obstacles placed here and there for every one of you. But when you can link with that spirit within and understand the great power of God the Father, then you have all the ammunition that you need in the fight against the negativity and the treachery that there is in your world, by those that misuse the power within themselves and then say that they have God's permission to bulldoze themselves forward, and to take over power from the people, from mankind itself.

And so, we want to give you that courage, we want to give you that understanding of the light, we want you to look at the work of John the Baptist and Jesus the Christ and those others that have come to walk the earth plane that have worn the badge of Spirit, never mind the label that they wore as to what religion it would become in the minds of man. You see, you have a thinking mind that is yours to control; you are able, all of you, to be channels for the spirit. You can go about your day to day living, giving of yourself and being able to see where there is a need in others that you may be able to help fulfil, as they disbelieve that there is a world of light and love. They do not wish to understand that the spirit continues, that death is nothing but rebirth, and so it is that you will always have those that come forward to demonstrate how the spirit can be used and utilized to the glory of God the Father.

And so, we say to you, my friends, fight the good fight, and good night and God bless.

GOOD EVENING to you, my friends, *(Congregation: Good evening, White Feather, welcome)* it is a pleasure to come and to talk with you.

And perhaps you would like to know that we have been waiting in the wings to deliver these words to you, because you have had a healing experience, shall we say, a workout tonight. So that you can, indeed, feel within you the power of the spirit. Because, you know, you all have your doubts, you all have your worries and your fears that can, indeed, hold you back.

Soon you will be celebrating, no doubt, your harvest services, as many religions do, at this time of year. You count your blessings, and the harvest has been gathered in in order to sustain physical life. And so, there are those in your world that do, indeed, suffer famine, and those countries that have much to offer in the way of sustenance and food for all humankind, but you know, it does not happen that it is shared throughout your world of matter. So, some go without and some have too much, and indeed much goes to waste.

And so, we would tell to you about the fruits and the vine, because when you look around your world you see devastation, you see those that are wanting power over others. You see fear, and those that want you to be fearsome of your world and the humankind within it. It makes you sad, it makes you depressed, it makes you unwell, and so we want you to realise that there is much work that goes on from the realms of light, from the realms of spirit, and through eons of time your Masters have come to tell to you all about your spiritual unfoldment and the fruits that you can bear, in your work, for the spirit. Nothing, you know, is ever wasted, and you may have trials and tribulations to face; all of you have to face losing your loved ones from the physical world, and so it is that you learn, through your experiences in life, and slowly but surely you have what you may term a spiritual awakening, when the fruits of the spirit are there for you to use. To bring to yourself peace, harmony and love, which is what your healing exercise was all about.

And so, you have had a taste of what it is to be in touch with yourself. Jesus walked the earth and worked bringing forward the light of God the Father, bringing forward the fruits that are there, for those that are willing to listen and understand all about the spirit within. And so it is that you, too, can work using your spirituality and the gifts that you bring forward in your day to day living. It is no use becoming spirituality aware and spirituality enlightened without you do the work in the name of God the Father, in the name of Love, for God is indeed love.

When you look around your world and see those that say they act in love and yet do murderous acts, it does not make sense. But you know, everybody that does good work reaps their rewards in the realms of spirit. They will feel that they have journeyed on, even though their physical life has been cut short, and sometimes in a barbaric and inhumane way. Have no fear for those individuals that have lost their lives in that way, because their life continues, and they are enlightened beings, and so they understand and they do not at all have any grudge against those that shortened their physical lives. Because, my friends, they are spirituality aware. Life cannot be taken away, life continues, just in a different state of being. Rest assured that we in the spirit world bring all that is needed to that individual that has lost their physical life, whether that be your loved one, your friend, or indeed, someone that you do not know. We want to bring to your world enlightenment that there is no death; we tell you those words every time we come to speak with you, but you see the human race tend to forget, and there are no martyrs, you know, to the spirit. The spirit will unfold and move on when the time is right for that individual to take those steps forward. And so, you know, you might be frightened by all that is going on in your world, but there is always a purpose, through everybody's life, in the physical, as there is when that life continues in the spiritual realms.

So, we thank you, indeed, for your prayers to those that have lost their physical lives; we welcome too, also, the prayers that you say for those that are inflicting fear on others, because they too need to be enlightened, because shall we just say that they are misusing their own spirituality. They are misguided, sometimes, in the way that they think with the logical mind, because of those that have tried to take control of your world. Let us just remind you that the Great Spirit that you call God is in control. At your harvest time you will give thanks to God for blessings of the earth and the world of nature. That continues whatever comes forth. You have had good weather also, and other places have not. Because you see it is always swings and roundabouts, because there are many that need to look within to find that spirituality and to work on their own spiritual pathway in life. So, as you have done in your healing work out, remember to look within, remember to give thanks to God the Father for all the blessings bestowed upon you. Because sometimes, you know, when you are in the darkness of despair and fear, that is when you are most likely to see the light of the spirit within you. And so we encourage you all to work with that light, to work with those in the spirit world that walk this earth plane with you, albeit unseen, but you are never alone. All those that have lost their lives, as we said, in those terrible circumstances, their spirit has been prepared for the transition, so do not fear. There is much, you know, to learn about those in your world that seem to want to only work in the darkness. And do not wish to work in the light. But we can tell to you that the light will dispel all darkness in time. But the world of matter is one where lessons are learnt but nothing is lost. So, rest assured that you're moving forward on your pathway as you should.

The fruits of your labours will be known to you and to others and more importantly to those in the spirit world, so that you will reap your rewards when you return back to the spirit world. You will have your own harvest, of that good work that you have done, the work that you have learnt has to begin within you. You have to work hard on yourself. It is not easy to practice meditation; it is not easy to practice love for yourself and for others. Because you are wanting things to be right for you as you see fit for you. And so, we want to expand your minds, we want to tell you about the vines with the fruits that appear there. Because there is always a way forward, there is never going back. What has happened in the past is left in the past as you realise the strength that is within you, the strength of the spirit. And so, you can begin, at any time, to take control of you. To allow those fruits to come forward, so that you may share with others your well-found knowledge of all those things that are spiritual, so that the light may continue to shine forth as it does from this Temple of Light. That is why we like to come here to talk with you. Because we feel at home, you see, in the energies that are within, that are held within, this building and you all contribute to that energy. Many of you, no doubt, come here when you are feeling a little low, when you are in need of healing, when you are in need of help, when you are need of understanding. All those things are fruits of the spirit. And that is why Jesus came to talk in that manner so that his followers, the disciples, could tell it to all those that were willing to listen. It is written down in the books, there is much knowledge within that book. Sometimes it can be heavy going to bring understanding that is why we are talking to you in this straightforward manner so that the mystery can disappear and you can begin to understand all about God the Father, Jesus the Son, and you being part of that life force that you call God. And so we say to you that is all that we need you to know but that you need to give thanks, to come and praise the name of God the Father, to come forward and thank God for all the blessings bestowed upon you. Even at the time, they may not have appeared to be a blessing but a curse. There is no such thing as a curse, my friends, because you will leave that behind that patch that is dull and seems to be there to destroy, when in fact it is there to put you back on the right path, the path of enlightenment, the path of truth, the path of love.

And so, we leave with you the love of God the Father, and say to you, good night and God bless.

Chapter Eight
Treforest SNU Church, Pontypridd

SUNDAY 31ST AUGUST 2014

GOOD EVENING to you, my friends, it is a pleasure to come and to talk with you.

And to bring to you some words that are going to assist you in your day to day living and your day to day understanding of life.

Because, you know, your world seems to be engulfed in darkness, for there is much turmoil and difficulty within many nations, and indeed sometimes, you know, you seem to be within yourselves in a little bit of turmoil, of, shall we say, indecision about life and indeed about your own spirituality and your own gifts of the spirit.

And so it is very important, you see, that we come to bring to you words, words that you may listen to, but words also that may encourage and give, what shall we say, food for thought, would be a good way of describing it, because, you know, you have to feed your physical bodies, do you not? You all have your favourite meals, your favourite food, indeed, your favourite drink, which I am sure is not water out of the tap, because there are other things more exciting, yes?; so it is that there are things too that are exciting within our realm of life, one of which is the ability to be able communicate to you on the earth plane.

Now, all of you have communication with the spirit world that will feed your soul. Whether you like it or not, you are all capable of receiving what we send to you, and that opening music talked to you about angels being at your side, and indeed that is true also, but you tell to yourselves when you are being inspired by the spirit world that you have, what you term, an overactive imagination. You are all guilty of that; you say it was my own mind telling me this and telling me that, and yes, indeed, you do have to keep control of your own mind, but you do that in your day to day living anyway, because you are always making decisions, you are deciding what you are going to do, whether you are going to do this, that or something else; it does not matter but you are deciding, you see, because you are in control of you, and that is good.

We in the spirit world may have a little control over our medium here this evening, to bring these words to you, but she has a mind that we have to work with, you know and so we have this understanding that she moves out to one side, and then we have a little bit of control, to bring to you what you need to understand about Spiritualism, about the spirit, about the God the Creator, about all things that sometimes seem to be a little mysterious to the world, because they are all seeking power, you know, and so one will fight another for power over, maybe land, maybe over the interpretation of various religious beliefs.

And so, we want you to be brave in your own

understanding, because as was said in the reading, when you face what you term death it is but rebirth of the soul. And that is you, the person that you truly are. You know you can disguise yourself by the clothes that you wear. You can change, and then people may not recognise you if you change to a different set of clothing that is different to what you would normally wear. Some people like to wear colourful things and other people like to keep them plain and simple. Because you all have your own individual tastes. Because you are individual people, so you all have your own individual ways of linking with the spirit world. But the spirit world will never leave you on your own as you see it. You will always be given guidance and help through your own being, you see. You all seek help from other people, because you have to cooperate one with the other. You have to be of service when you look at the spirit within you and understand that life will continue be what may.

And for those that do not understand or want to give time to understanding that the spirit will move on into a new life, then that is for them. You do not have to go out and preach the principles of Spiritualism, but we would ask that you live by the principles of Spiritualism, because you can interpret them as you may find is best for you. You only have seven, and you know, there are always rules and regulations within your world, and they just pile on one after the other to make life difficult, but one being that you have to stick to a speed limit on your roads, and it varies depending upon which road you are travelling, so it can be confusing, but to have a good journey then you have to take notice of the speed limit, of the signs, and so it is within your own spiritual unfoldment: you are on a journey; you have to go by the speed limits.

And you know, there are too many that start their unfoldment and then want to speed it along as quick as they can, you know, because they feel this power and this energy of the spirit within. But we like to set you speed limits so that you can take it at your own pace; that will mean that you understand all about your own self, the person that you are. Because it does not matter what religious belief you would like to call yourself, or what you follow in the way of understanding, because it is only words. You are all equal, you see, because you are all spirit, here and now. It won't be that you become a spiritual being when the body fails you, and you have reached that point that you call death. And so it is that we want to encourage you to work with your gifts of healing, with your gifts of clear seeing. It is important, you know, because you also sense, you can all perhaps go house hunting one day and step over a doorstep and know that you could not live in that particular building. Because you sense, you use your senses. Your animal kingdom use their senses to a greater extent than perhaps you do, but it is all of the same essence, you see, because you are all part of life.

It is important, therefore, that you take responsibility for yourself, one of the principles entitled 'Personal Responsibility'. And you know that the principles were given by a gentleman called Robert Owen, through the mediumship of Emma Hardinge Britten, and Robert Owen was also a founder member of the Co-operative Society. And only days ago there was a meeting for them to change some of the fundamentals of that society, because it is now not as, what shall we say, upbeat as it once was, and so it is a little bit in the doldrums with regard to finance and business in your everyday world. And even that has had to change, you see, so we are not saying to change your principles, but we are saying that you need to live by those very same principles to understand and get a grip on what Spiritualism is truly about. Too many people diversify, I think is the word that you would use, and do all sorts of things that just focus the mind so that they link with the spirit within to bring healing forward, to bring communication from your loved ones, and indeed to give to you futuristic events to keep you motivated, to keep you thinking about what the spirit world is all about. But we do not need all those tools, we just need you to have an open mind, to, indeed, have an open heart, because your spirit is going to give, and then you are going to receive more and more from those in the spirit world that connect themselves to you, the light that you carry, the light that you are. But you cannot be hidden by the persona that you wish to give off to others or by what clothes you wear to identify or indeed to un-identify yourself within your circle of friends and family and work colleagues and the like. And so, we encourage you all to understand that that spirit within you is going to keep you going forever and ever. It is very difficult to understand that word, eternity, but it means no beginning and no end and so you are the person that you are. You are the person that the spirit is.

And so, you see, there are many that mistrust others, mistrust themselves. And that is why we give to you this idea that you must trust in yourself, in that essence of spirit that you are. Because it is important that you realise that you are spirit, that you are not just a physical body that when the time comes will return to the earth and then, you see, there is nothing more. Because there is so much more; that is why that it is important that we ask you to take up arms, not in the way of fighting each other, but to be positive, to be wanting to move forward in your life.

You may read many books, because there are those that are written that were inspired by people from the spirit world, and they have always something positive to say to you. There is too much doom and gloom in your world, and it is mankind, itself, that is bringing this to the fore. Because even in times of war, you know, there is much work done with people giving of themselves and being able to help those that are suffering because they have been in the range of the missiles, of the guns, of the bombs. And you know, even in war times there is an element of peace being brought forward all the time, when those go out and help, even those that are struck by famine and their lives are cut short, there are many that go out in their physical being to aid. And you know everybody wants to give of money, but what we ask is that you give of yourselves also. Because sometimes that is more than money can buy.

And so, your world is, indeed, commercialised, shall we put it that way, and evolves around, or revolves around, having to have a certain amount of money to exist. And there are those that receive from your state, but shall we say, think it is their right to receive and then they do not give, and we do not mean just of money. So, it is important when you reach difficult times in your life, because you all will, that you realise that it is about giving and receiving, because some people who may be healers within Spiritualism, they always do the giving of the healing but they forget about receiving for themselves, because we can't have all our healers and mediums and people within the Spiritualist church worn out because they are giving all of the time. In that giving you have to learn about receiving from others and from the spirit world also, and so it is a two-way street, you see. That is why we use that analogy, again, of driving on your roads. Because, you know, even if you do not drive yourself you are in vehicles, whether they be buses or trains or indeed planes, but you do use these things to take you on a journey within your physical world. And so, we want to take on a journey within the spiritual realms of life, so that you can see and understand all about another dimension of life, where power is equal to all, not one person, not one nation has power over others, because that is what happens in your world; you all vie for power, you see, and want to control one and all.

Even the Divine Creator that you call God does not want to control by power. They want cooperation by power, yes, to bring the two worlds together, because, really, you know, the world is your oyster to stand up and be counted and talk about your understanding that the spirit will live on. It does not matter how you reach the spirit world; reach it you will, because it is the same for everyone in your world. They will eventually move on into that new dimension of life, new to them but part and parcel of life as a whole.

And so, that should help those that grieve the loss of

their loved ones, because, you know, it is but a transition. It is not really a loss, it is not a loss into oblivion, it is just the loss of the physical presence, which, indeed, sometimes can be very difficult to deal with. But deal with it, is part of your earthly life, my friends, and so we want to tell to you that if you can spread the word that there is no death, that the spirit of the individual will move forward in life, then that should help many a person that struggles, that comes to terms with changes in their lives. Change, those people do not wish to confront, but indeed, life changes minute to minute, second to second, day to day, month to month and year to year.

And so, you have every opportunity to use your gifts of the spirit; it does not matter what happened yesterday, today is a new day, you can start it afresh whenever you like with this new understanding that the spirit is part of you, the individual. So we give to you the understanding of the power of God, the power of the spirit that is within you, and with that power and with those angels walking with you, those guides and helpers, those family and friends, you cannot fail but to achieve. And that is what we want you to understand: power is yours, my friends. You have to use the power of your spirit wisely. You have to take responsibility for what you do, for how you do it, because it is in your motive that is really important. It is no good helping somebody because you expect something in return. It is good that you wish to help others by being of service to God the Father; that is all that we ask of each one of you.

There is a supreme, Divine being that you call God, that we call the power of the universe, that we call the

Great White Spirit – it does not matter what name you put to this energy – that is the energy of life, that is eternal. So, use that power that you have wisely, do not use it to inflict your ways on others, because that is not good, you are just exerting power over. Feed your spirit, just as you would feed your body with your favourite food; feed your spirit with the understanding that God is good, that the Creator is there for you, that those in the spirit world are there for you to help you, to bring you light, to bring you understanding of truth.

It may sound that we are just using words, but it is through words, through thoughts that we can inspire and uplift, through music also, because you all sat very quietly and listened and went along with that music that would put you into a meditative state as long as you wanted to enter that meditative state; we do not push you to do anything that is not important to you, because co-operation is the best thing that can happen between your world and ours. And if that law of co-operation, cause and effect, was seen a little more widely in your world, then wars would cease, famine would cease, because you would all be co-operative one with the other on a grand scale, grander than you can imagine, and then peace would reign, you see.

So, all that we ask is that you find for now peace within yourselves, and that will aid us in bringing peace to your world, your material world, because peace reigns in our world of the spirit, it reigns eternal and that is why we like to come forward and to give you some ideas that maybe, in your terms, 'outside of the box' in which you normally think, the range you normally think, and so we ask that you do expand your mind, you do expand your heart, and then you will be of service and your life will be, what you may term, fulfilled. And so, take that power and use it wisely, my friends, and then you will be servants of God the Father, the Creator of all life.

And we say to you, good night, and God bless.

Chapter Nine

Weston Super Mare, SNU Church, Stafford Road

SUNDAY 23RD JUNE 2013

GOOD EVENING to you, my friends, it is a pleasure to come and to talk with you.

For, you know, all of you have many questions, and you are seeking answers, and that is good as far as we are concerned in the spirit world. It is important, you see, that you do take seriously your spiritual pathway in life. Because your material world and the spiritual realms and your understanding of both should be parallel one to the other.

The reading, of course, was quite long, and yet you summed it all up in the hymn that you sang next, 'A Melody of Love', because you have to be in harmony with yourself, with your thinking mind and your spiritual essence, that is the true person that you are. For it is the spirit that is going to move on in your life to give you eternal life, because, you know, one of your principles is that you have Eternal Progress open to every Human Soul. But we must congratulate all of you, for, you know, you are looking for answers to questions, for life in your material world can be difficult and tedious at times, just to use two descriptives of life in your world of matter.

And so, we come to allay your fears and to put to one side all those things that trouble you. You only have to switch on your radio or your television or your internet to find numerous things that are going worry you about what is happening within your world, and the spirituality within mankind seems to be something that is unattainable, and yet, you know, we would encourage you all to look at your own spirituality, because it is love that binds you altogether.

It is God the Creator that gives to you all unconditional love in equal measure; not one of you has more of less of it, it is yours for the taking, yours for the understanding. We know that you get tired physically and mentally, but spiritually you are alive and well and vibrating as you should. Because, you see, your physical body confines the spirit, and it is the spirit that is the essential ingredient, shall we say. In your world you seem to have, what shall we say, lots and lots of programmes on cooking and food and the nutritional value of such to keep your body sustained. Well, we would talk to you about spiritual aspects of life, to keep your spirit sustained as it struggles on through this existence within the material physical world, because, you know, you are all journeying along the same pathway of life.

You are all making decisions, all of the time. You all have the correct ingredients, you know, for enjoying life, but you have to be in touch with your true self, with your spirit, and that enables you then to be in touch with the spiritual realms where your loved ones and your friends and your guides and helpers have a life also; and you know, part of their work is to tell to you the truths of life, to give you help and guidance, but you know, you have to ask, it cannot just be thrown at you. You know, when you are doing your cookery, then you are going to have ingredients listed, and you are not just going to put everything into the bowl and hope for the best, although some of you do! But you know, in a recipe it is measured out so that you can get the results that should make for a fine meal to undertake, and so it is that we give you all the relevant ingredients that you need for your spiritual well being so that your spirit is fed, so that you are able to understand all about eternal life. All about the gifts that you have been given that have been bestowed upon you by God the Father, the Great Creator, the Great Spirit that essence of life itself.

And so, we would encourage you to ask all of these questions and to work with your psychic faculties so that you may link and have knowledge and understanding through personal experience of the spirit realms. There are too many in your world that would wish to conjure up fear of that very communication that is yours for the understanding of; it is personal to each one of you, and so, you see you have steps to take forwards in your life, and as you take on board the essence of the message, then you are not going to fear the world that you consider to be unknown, the world that runs parallel to your physical world. For the two interpenetrate but exist in different states of vibration, and so there is science involved in this, there is a religious aspect also. And you know, you talk about Spiritualism as being a philosophy, a science and a religion, and so you see, you are thinking all of time, and it is good that you are able to ask these questions of those in the spirit realms.

The next part of your service is going to be communication from your loved ones and friends. And that may be what draws you in to a church such as this, because you want to know that they are fine, that they are well, that their existence continues, that their spirit continues in that world beyond matter. And yet, you know, you have to really take on board philosophical aspects of life, so that you can face all adversity, for your life will never be plain sailing, there will always be rough waters here and there. It is the school room of life, this material world, and you are all learning from your lessons, and doing it very well, we may add, if you then look within yourself to find strength, to find courage, to find harmony and peace and to find love that passes all understanding. Because, you see, all those things are there for the taking.

We do not ask that you have strings attached to accept God's love, that is eternal. All that we ask is you take on board your understanding of truth. There are many myths, of course, in your world, there are many fairy tales told to you, especially as children, and then when you realise that some of those things are not true, then it is upsetting and you lose faith, you see. And we want you to have faith in yourselves and in the spirit realms, because that is the truth. And it is important that you take this on board, for healing can be administered to you.

You know, there are many that think that the physical body is all that is in life. And so, they worry and despair when there is no need. To take on board that your spirit has eternity in which to progress is good news. You are all equal, as we said, in the essence of the spirit, and so it is that you can choose whether or not to work with those gifts that have been bestowed upon you.

It is not a mystery; it is a given that you can utilise your gifts and work as a channel for the spiritual world. And in so doing you will find that you are moving forward, that life is less arduous, that you are able to understand what life is about, and by your actions and by your thoughts other people that may not have your understanding of a spiritual essence will realise that you glow and burn a light that can be seen by them, because they want to know what makes you tick, that you are able to cope so admirably in your life. It is the essence of your spirit, my friends, and so we would encourage you all to look at your pathway to see where it is that you are going. Because, you know, you do not become a spiritual being at that point of death, you are a spiritual being here and now.

We want you to be inspired, we want you to take notice of your inner being. We want you to look and see, we want you to have answers to your questions, we want you to be an instrument for the spirit world, and then, you see, your world will begin to alter. There will be this great spiritual upliftment that you will find, and it will give you the impetus to move on, to ask more questions, to find more answers so that you can be a servant of the Great Spirit that you call God.

That is all that we ask: is that you serve the spirit, the spirit that is you, and in so doing, the spirit world will aid you in your endeavours, because it is a privilege for us in the spirit world to have channels that we may use to bring forward the power of the spirit, to bring forward the power of clear seeing, to bring forward the power of the laying on of hands and the administering of healing, and so it is that your world will evolve slowly but surely towards the light of God, that great eminence that is the Creator of all things, and so we encourage one and all to take those steps slowly but surely into the light of the spirit, and to use what knowledge you have to encourage others to do the same.

Be positive; do your best is all that we ask of you, and you cannot fail. You may feel that you have no energy, that you have no strength, but you know, when you allow the spirit within to guide you, and you go with that intuition that is yours then you cannot fail. You can only move forward in bigger and bigger steps so that you are always working in the light of God the Father.

Within your Spiritualism you have just seven principles that are open to your own personal interpretation, and yet they will keep you on the straight and narrow of your spiritual unfoldment, so take heed, read them, see what you think is the meaning behind them, and you cannot fail. You have all that you need within you, but it is good to come together collectively from to time to time to talk amongst yourselves, to ask questions of one another and of the spirit world so that you can see that you are growing in stature. All that we ask is that you face your world in humility, knowing that you are encased in the love of God the Father, that you can be a servant to God the Father, and in so doing you will transform yourself, and others also will wish to follow your light of love and truth. So, that is all that we ask that you work in the light of God. That you work in the light of spirit, that you are able to move forward so that you can see that you are doing God's work and being a good and faithful servant in the face of all adversity that you might have to deal with; it will not stop you, it will only help you to see that you are in control, that you are about God's work.

And so, we say to you, my friends, good night and God bless.

GOOD EVENING to you, my friends, it is a pleasure to come and to talk with you.

And to, yes, bring you some upliftment within yourselves as we endeavour to touch your spirituality. The real you, the person that you are of spirit, you see. Because you are on your own individual pathway of unravelling your own spiritual potential, and it will not be suddenly that it all happens, for it is a gradual process, and that is why you spend some time in your earthly years with your spirit encased within your body. And, you know, it is prompting you all of the time to go forward to bring forward that light, that light of God's love, and the expression that is that of the spiritual essence of life.

For with each one of you, you have those that attach themselves to you, whether they be family, friends or those that you have not given a name to, but there are spiritual people that are there from the spirit realms, that attach themselves to you to guide you through your life, not by talking directly to you, but by standing beside you, most of the time unseen, but prompting you to go forward in your understanding of life and all the issues that are thrown up in your material world. And yet it does seem dark and gloomy to you, some of the time, and when your news is given to you, you know, in a certain regard, it is censored, because how many people give to you good news? It is always doom and gloom, and that does indeed deflate your enthusiasm, deflate your positivity, so that doubt creeps in to your spiritual understanding and so it is that we need, all of the time, channels that we can use to show to you things that are positive, to show to you how the power of the spirit can indeed move mountains, you know. Because sometimes you are given tasks to do that seem, at the outset, insurmountable for you the individual.

But, nevertheless, when you put your mind to things, you accomplish a great deal, and you know, just to give a kind word, a smile, a thought to somebody else, then you are doing the work of the spirit and the work of God the Father. And so it is that you understand that you have to take small steps in your own lives to accomplish great things, and when you return to the spirit world, you will see all of your accomplishments, and you will not have failed in any regard. You may think that you have not been given enough time on the earth, or that your loved ones have not been given enough time, especially if they transcend to the spirit world at an early age in your earth years. Then you think that their life has been cut short, but we can tell to you that their life has been the allotted span, that was required for their spirit to learn certain aspects of a physical life, and once that has been accomplished, the next stage is to transcend the world of matter back to the spiritual realms of light and love. And to be in an existence that works unceasingly to bring that light, into your earth environment, and you know, there are too many that are warmongers, shall we say, in your world and are not happy unless there is friction between this, that and the other. Whereas, in point of fact, what we all pray for, in your world and ours, is peace. And what we would say to you is that you have firstly to find peace within your very being, and sometimes that is difficult when you are living your life in the physical world, in the world of materialism and you get caught up in what you may term, the rat race of life. But we make allowances for all that you do and do not do, because you have open your heart and your mind to the influence of those that walk with you to help you along the way.

Too many complain that when they are in need, they do not seem to have the spirit world beside them. And yet, you know, there is that famous poem called 'Footprints' that explains that when you were in need there was only one set of footprints in the sand because that was when God was carrying you, and it's God's footprints that are there. And so when you think that the spirit world are moving, you forward in your understanding, in the giving of yourself in service to the Great Spirit, then you cannot fail, and you will be carried forward in your life and you will surmount all those obstacles before you. You will surmount the tragedy of losing a loved one or friend from the physical world.

But remember they are not lost in the spiritual world, they are alive and well and have a life that continues, and so it is that you give to them every opportunity of communicating with you, because, you know, they are happy at the release from the physical bonds of life. They are happy back in our world, and yet they have time to support you, to give you strength, to give you their love, that, of course, is unconditional. And so, we need you all to spread that message, because too many are in fear of the unknown. They think that for the spirit to live on is a fallacy whereas, in fact, it is a truth. A truth of spiritual understanding of the spiritual laws, for the spirit is an energy, and energy will not die, it will only transform itself. Look at your caterpillars, that transform into beautiful butterflies, and have a different life altogether.

And so it is that the life in the spiritual realms is different, it's a different aspect altogether of understanding, and with your logical, thinking mind, things do not make sense, but when you link with that spirit within, you will understand that those loved ones live on, that they have life anew. We were going to say a new life, which is true, to a greater or lesser degree, because it depends on their spiritual understanding when they were on the earth. And so, you can always expand your spiritual understanding and your spiritual awareness, and that is what we ask of each individual. You do not have to belong to any organisation to do just that.

Within your world there are too many that seem to be in your news today, radicalised into understanding that they have to be a martyr to God, in order to have eternal life. It is so sad that this happens in your world. There is so many, you see, that have this spiritual understanding that is misplaced by those that want to gain power over your world, the earth world. And it will not be and cannot be allowed to happen. And that is why we ask you to use a modern phrase, to become workers of light, or light workers, because you have to have the right motive, you see, and that motive has to be one of unconditional love. You do not do something for someone else in order to gain in the material sense; you do it in order that you bring love forward. Because it is love in action or, shall we say, spirit in action that brings your world around to that spiritual understanding of the Continuous Existence of the Human Soul, and that is the truth. That is the beginning and the end of the matter.

And so it is that there is much to be learnt within your material, physical world about life, about the continuation of life. About the messages and communication from your loved ones and the ministry of angels, because we are all busy in our world bringing that light forward to dispel the darkness and fear of many in your world. And so it is that you have to be understanding of your own spirituality; you all have a passion for life, you all want to experience love from God the Father, and that is all that it is about, in essence, for your spirit within will respond to God's love and then you will be on what we may term a mission in life, to help yourself, and then helping others in your own understanding, and with your own belief system in the fact that the spirit has an eternity with which to progress. Which means that you cannot fail; failure is not in the plan of God the Father. Positivity is all that you need to keep hold of as you go forward, ignoring all that is happening in the wider world and concentrating what is happening within you, within your own communication with others, within your own communication with the spirit world. And so let us all march forward together in the light of the Great Spirit, of God's light, for there are many Masters that have come to the earth to show you the way of the spirit, not to fight one with the other over a certain belief structure, but to come together in unity of love for one another, for the spirit world that continues to serve. Whatever you get up to in your life, they will not fail you. They will always support and encourage you to go forward, to not be a fight as some of these extremists seem to think that it is. It will not happen in a blinding flash, as was said in that reading, but each one can contribute to bringing that light and being a channel for the spirit realms to use, so that people can be trustworthy of themselves, and know that they are on a sure footing to channel the energy of the love of God the Father.

And so, we say to you, my friends, blessings from the spirit realms of life and please take forward that upliftment and that positivity that will have touched your spirit just because you have congregated here this evening in this house of worship and praise and work of healing and light.

And so, we say to you, good evening, and God bless.

GOOD EVENING to you, my friends, it is a pleasure to come and to talk with you.

And indeed, to offer you some light, shall we say, in the darkness of your world, where you seem to be consumed, from time to time, with fear that has been mentioned in the songs that you have sung, in addition to the reading that was chosen. And you see, our channel did not have access to the hymns that were chosen, and that is how we work to help you in your daily lives. To touch your own auric field, to help you to make decisions that you find difficult, to face things that you are fearful of, because your life in the physical world will change, and indeed, it can be constant change, because nothing ever stays the same.

You grow from your childhood into your adolescence into your adulthood, and you face many different challenges that are yours to face, for each one of you here is indeed an individual, and you can decide that you have certain ambitions, and why not? And yet you sometimes feel that you do not reach those ambitions that you felt were right for you, because you have been diverted along the way. We welcome all you enlightened souls that would wish to explore your own spirituality, your own spiritual essence, and give you encouragement to move forward, to be of service so that you can dispel the fears of your mind, of your material mind, that perhaps sometimes will hold you back from experimentation with your own link with the spirit world.

Many young children have a natural ability to link with the spirit world, and when they are brave enough to say to you of their experiences sometimes, they are not, what shall we say, encouraged. They are told that it is their imagination running away with them, when indeed they are having their own communication with that world that is beyond that of matter, beyond that of the physical And they do not have a fear, it is the adults that do not understand, that are holding back and instilling fear into the young ones. It can be like that some of the time.

So, we would tell to you that we do indeed wish to dispel fear in your mind, because that fear builds up and creates barriers between that world of enlightenment, that world of light and love, the world of the spirit realms and you, the individual, that is spirit here and now.

There is no division, you see, you will not become angelic beings just because you leave your physical body. You will be the same person that you are, but you will become more enthusiastic about the spiritual aspect that you are and the spiritual aspects that are to be experienced. You may leave the world of matter tired and weary because your physical body has become that way over time, and yet your spirit within that moves forward will be vibrant, will be full of life, will be enthusiastic to continue the life that is there. You will meet up with those friends and loved ones that have departed the physical world before you, and it brings much joy to you and to them. Because they can be considered to have been onlookers in your life, for within Spiritualism you talk of Personal Responsibility, and it is so that you have to take responsibility for you yourself. You may ask advice from this one and that one, but you have to make your own decisions, and so it is in our world of light, and as you say, love.

Because the essence of your spirit is indeed love, and with that love you can be of service to others. It would not seem that way when you look into your world that is becoming ever decreasingly smaller because of media and technology. You can see what is going on in the far corners of the world, and some of it is very, very disturbing to you, the individual. You know you do have on that remote the off button that you can press to keep all that out of your mind when you come to overload from all that is bombarded at you.

Because the news, you know, is not very often good, and there is always tragedy, there is always something happening that is eating at your heart strings because you are sensitive, my friends, the spirit within you makes you a sensitive individual, a sensitive being and so you are bombarded with some of the things that are negative in your world, and that will instil fear into you. Well, we want to tell you that there is nothing to fear at all. You may grieve, of course, because that is a human emotion when your loved ones pass through that veil of death to the spirit world of life, and that is natural for you to do so. But you are grieving for yourselves, for that soul is moving on and that life is exciting and wonderful, and it is good for them to see the world as it is, the world of the spirit, the world that continues to give life to your spiritual self, and the aspect that is the real you, the spirit within. That is why we want to dispel fear. We want to give you the truth that life continues.

You talk of God the Father, you talk of the Brotherhood of Man because, believe or believe it not, you are all equal in the essence that you are spirit. You

246

may have different physicality of your bodies, of your skin, of your shape, of your size most of which does not fit to what you would want, but that is what you have. And so, you have to be realistic in your life, and as soon as you allow positivity into your mind then all these barriers of fear will just disintegrate before your very eyes. It sounds very simple as we tell it to you in this way, but of course life can be problematic, it can be disappointing, it can be indeed harrowing, but it is just for a short time in the greater scheme of life that you are, the spirit that you are is encased within the physical body which is very limiting to the spirit inside.

But you are on a journey of life, a journey of learning, and as long as you do not fear, then you are going to walk forward with great strides and you are going to be able to handle whatever life puts in your pathway. Because it is through that trying that you indeed do move forward in your understanding about life itself. You know, sometimes you wish that you could go back in your age but know the knowledge that you have at an older time, but you know, if you had that knowledge when you were young you may not have taken any notice of what you truly knew. That is all part of understanding the spirit that you are.

Silver Birch was using a channel to give the truths of life and indeed of death. And as he said fear is only negativity, so as soon as you look positively at things then the whole situation changes and you have much strength of mind, of character, of spirit to fulfil your life and learn more and more about the truths that are there for you to seek, that are there for you to understand and learn about.

Much has been written in many books about the truth and the light indeed in there for you to work with. We invite you always to test the spirit and to understand that you are more than the physical person that you think that you are.

So, indeed it is important to bring youngsters into a church and environment such as this, so that they can look within and find that spiritual essence that is theirs to use, to understand, and to be a channel for those in the spirit world who need a voice upon your earth plane. Because, you see, the truths need to be told, because too many are fanatical about what they believe.

Too many that believe the truth sit back and do not work with the spirit world as a channel, but many work with their own spirit and work in environments that are not conducive to a pleasant life, because they have to endure much hardship. Needless to say, your world continues to progress; although fear is instilled in mankind, it brings about a great deal of negativity, so we would leave with you, this evening, the positivity that is there within your spiritual being. We want you to take charge, we want you to take personal responsibility, we want you to link with the spirit world and send your thoughts so that you can be able to see the power of thought, the power of spirit in action.

You have endeavoured, this evening, to send your thoughts out for healing, to send your thoughts out for yourself and each one of you should leave this sanctuary feeling uplifted, feeling better than when you walked in through the doors, because it is spiritual nourishment that is needed within your world of matter, so that that fear is, indeed, dispelled and you can move on positively in your life, looking towards God the Creator for all the power and energy that you need, irrespective of what dilemma or problem you are facing in your life.

Communication is the key – communication between individuals, communication between the spirit world and you as individuals – and then you have the key, my friends, to success. You have the key, my friends, to peace. You have the key to love and life. Please take charge and move on and help yourselves, and in doing so you will be able to help others. That is what we want you to do, and take away the fear of death, which is but a transition into new life.

We say to you, my friends, good night and God bless.

Chapter Ten
Ystalyfera, SNU Church, Ystalyfera, Swansea

SUNDAY 15TH SEPTEMBER 2013

GOOD EVENING to you, my friends, it is a pleasure to come and to talk with you and to bring forward those words of encouragement that you all need, from time to time, because, you know, you are all questioning the spirit world.

We in our world are bombarded with questions from all of you, but we would have it no other way, because you are seeking to understand the power of the spirit within you. Because it is the spirit that gives you eternal life, as we said in the opening prayer. The reading spoke about power and the power of the spirit that is within you, the individual. It is the power of the spirit that gives you life eternal.

And so, you see, your life is continuous, and that, of course, is one of the principles within your Spiritualism. We would tell to you that you have a journey to make in your world, and to run parallel with your spiritual unfoldment; then you are truly finding peace within yourself, because the material world and that of the spiritual realm should run parallel one to the other, and then indeed, you will find peace within yourself.

All of you have minds that run away with you from time to time. Because, you know, it is very difficult to keep that mind of yours quiet. Because, you see, you are always thinking, you are always wanting to do your very best in life. Because there are many hurdles and obstacles that you have to overcome, and there are too many in your world that grieve for the loss of the physical body of their loved ones and friends, and so the message that we have to give out is to tell to you that the spirit will continue, that the life that you loved will continue, of that loved one that is precious to you and to us also in the spirit world.

Because you will, of course, mourn the loss of the physical presence, because that physical presence is important to you in the physical world, but too many dismiss the promptings of their own mind and spirit, because they think it is their imagination running away with them when they have thoughts of the loved one that they have lost from the physical world. But in truth, it is that they can still communicate with you as individuals through your thought processes, and sometimes through the dream state whilst you are sleeping, and your body and mind is resting from the rigours of daily life. That is the truth, that is the truth that you should be shouting from the roof tops, you know.

It is important within Spiritualism that you remember that it is all about proving survival of the spirit, not all about telling the future. Past and the present and the future indeed are all in one as far as we are concerned. What we are concerned about is the development of your spirituality, so that when your spirit returns to the spirit world you have overcome many obstacles and your light is strong. So that you have progressed, during that time that you have spent encased within your physical body, and sometimes, you know, the physical body can house that spirit, but the spirit is not always allowed expression, because not many people look within themselves and use the gifts of the spirit that are theirs, given to them freely by God the Father, the Creator of all life, and so that is, my friends, your responsibility: to look within yourself, to be honest with yourself.

You may look into a mirror, we tell this very often to people, and you look and see the physical reflection that you are. You study it closely, some of you, and decide that you do not like this, or you do not like that, or something else you would rather change, and yet you see you are not looking at the spirit, the true self, that can be seen in our world but remains hidden from those who are not willing to open their hearts and their minds to the existence of the spirit realm of life and the spirit that is the true person that you are.

And so it is quite simple, you know: you all have racing minds, as we have said; not many have time to sit in the peace and the quiet within themselves, but this, my friends, can be acquired if you set just a little time aside on the daily basis. There are many Masters that have walked your earth and demonstrated to you that the spirit can be strong, that the spirit can do miraculous work. That the spirit will allow you freedom of expression, that the spirit within will give you strength and courage to get you through many a problem that is in front of you. But you know, we do not always understand how that power of the spirit guards us and guides us and moves us forward. You have sung about peace. And you know, when you truly look and see and use the spiritual essence of yourself, then you will find a profound peace, and others will be amazed at how you cope with the challenges of life in the material world. And so, you can lead by example because you have faith, you have trust, in the spirit world. And in the truth that there is no death, for in our world it is a rebirth and you begin a new chapter within your life that will continue for an eternity. And so, you have an eternity with which to progress, and so we would ask that you look and see that things in your world can be accomplished little by little. You do not have to see things way into the future; today is a new day, tomorrow will be a new day, for you to take charge of yourself and your life and of your spiritual unfoldment. And then you will flourish as an individual. You can pass on your knowledge to all those who are ready to listen, but you cannot enforce your knowledge and your understanding on anyone else. They have to come to the conclusion themselves: that life does not make sense if there was only the physical aspect to it. And so you see, to understand the spirit they seem to be deep and difficult; but in point of fact, we are just saying to you that you are capable of many things, of working with that spirit within, of refining your gifts bestowed upon you by God the Father, for you know, you are all a brotherhood, in the fact. that all human life has a spiritual essence. Indeed, all life does, you know, but there is the animal kingdom to consider and the kingdom of nature also.

The logo within Spiritualism talks of Nature, Light and Truth. So allow that light of the spirit to guide you forward and know that you are understanding the truths of the spirit, and then you see, you can combine it in your natural world of materialism, and then the message will surely go forward; the power that you have, my friends, is great. You have to harness that power and use it wisely. You began this service by blending your voices in song; you sent out thoughts to all those that are in need and even to those that are unknown to you. The healing ambassadors will work with that need with their healing energy of love. So all that we ask of you is that you use your gifts wisely, that you listen to that power within you. You may call it intuition; go with it, my friends, and do the work of the spirit and that of the Father that you call God. And then, you cannot fail, so we ask that you keep positive, that you spread the word to those that you meet, to those who you know are ready to listen. It is important, you see, that you are in control of your life. We in the spirit world can guide you, for you all have guides and helpers and family and friends that draw close to you at times when you are in need. But sometimes you do not realise just how close those in the spirit are with you. It is a world of thought, and so we are just a thought away. So use your mind positively, use your spirit to strengthen yourself and to allow that light to carry forward, to inspire others, to look for the truth and to gain in understanding of spiritual values.

You all have a great power within to use wisely so that you can bring forward that message, message of the love of God the Father, message of the love that binds you together with those that you loved and who loved you. The tie that binds is not broken at that point that you call death, it is always there giving you strength, bringing you courage, bringing you hope and joy and peace.

And so, my friends, we would leave those thoughts with you so that you can exercise your mind from time to time. Send us those thoughts; we are always willing to answer any questions that you may have, because in questioning, you see, and sending your thoughts out to the spirit world, you are going forward, you are expanding your mind, you are expanding your heart and your soul, and all that is called progression towards the Godhead.

And so we would say to you, my friends, good night and God bless.

GOOD EVENING to you, my friends, it is a pleasure to come and to talk with you.

And to bring to you those words of inspiration, those words of upliftment, because it is a fact that you all have many, many, many thoughts that go through your mind, both day and night. Because you are all questioning things that you are aware of in your day to day living, and many question those things from the world unseen.

There are many in your world that grieve when they lose their loved ones, and the physical presence is no more, but yet do not have the courage to look at the world unseen or indeed to God and spirit for answers that perplex them. And you know, the message within Spiritualism is indeed that you should interpret the seven principles with your own logical, thinking mind. Because those seven principles are open to interpretation as you would wish, as you would understand. It is important, therefore, that as you read out those principles you realised that there was substance in what you were reading, in what those seven principles say to you, the individual. There is no creed, no dogma, nothing that is going to hinder you, because those principles should make sense to you.

In fact, those principles were given from the spirit world through the mediumship of Emma Hardinge Britten, and you know, the person or the spirit entity that gave those principles to her was Robert Owen, a gentleman who founded the Co-Op Movement, that helped many through those days when there was not much that good about the material world. But what was good, in his opinion, was to be shared amongst everybody, workers and customers alike. For if you shopped in that environment then you were suitable for what they would call a dividend, and so it is a bit like what you would think of the spirit world, no doubt, because as you give of yourself, so you receive. As you sow, so you reap, as was said in that reading.

And so it is that things have to be logical, that answers have to be found for you, the individual. It is important, therefore, that you open your mind, that you open your heart, that you give of that spirit within you, because it is the spirit that gives you life that will last for an eternity. And this physical world is but a blink of the eye, so to speak, in the greater scheme of life. Those that face, and you all will, the tragedy that you call death, is but rebirth in our world, and that individual person that is no longer within the physical world moves forward into life anew, in the realms of light and love. And then, you see, that means that the spirit itself has transformed, has moved on.

That is the greatest message that Spiritualism can give you, because, when you grieve, your thoughts are dark and dismal, and you feel that there is no way forward. That is why we wish to dispel that belief that is held by so many in your world. You see that it is important to have a voice, to be able to inspire, uplift and help those in your world that do not know which way to turn when grief strikes them, and strike the individual it will do, at some time or another, and mostly when it is inconvenient, as you would say, in your modern day speaking.

You have greater means in your modern world of communication, and yet you throw out the inspiration given to you from the spirit world as overactive imagination. You have some excuse, whereas in point of fact the spirit world and those that walk with you, family, friends and guides alike, are constantly trying to impress your mind to see the positive, to understand that your loved ones and friends live on in a different state of vibration. That is the only difference between the course vibration of the physical world where it is all seen. What you see is what you believe. What you don't see, you tend not to believe. And that in itself is a fallacy.

All that we ask of you is that you seek answers, is that you seek the truths of the spirit. It said in that reading that your understanding of the truth can change but the truth is the same because there is no death. That is the truth that too many are unwilling to accept. Because they think that the spirit world is something that is intangible and that does not exist.

And so you have much work to do in your world, because, you know, even if you have convinced yourself by your searching and your questioning, then doubt comes in if you may be discussing your beliefs with somebody that is not of the same, what shall we say, mind-set. Communication is a natural occurrence between your world and ours, and you know, in your world, you all use, or the majority of you use, modern technology, keeping in touch by text or email or phone, and yet still you do not always communicate with your family and friends to a high degree. It is simple to send this, that or the other, and indeed sometimes to send the message to the wrong person. And so it is, in the spirit world we may use you to take a message on to somebody else, because they are not as brave as you to be in an environment where messages can be given, where gifts of the spirit are used and utilised to bring that love forward, to give hope, to give understanding to all those in need.

You began your service with healing, and that is good for us, because we know that you are willing to change your state of thinking, your state of vibration, to set aside just a few moments to think of others, and included in that, of course, is the natural world of nature. The natural world in which the animal kingdom reside, the natural world in which you human race reside, that doesn't look too good from where we are standing in the spirit world, because there is much trouble and strife, there is much war and turmoil and famine, and all those things that are troublesome to your thoughts that may keep you awake at night with worry.

All the things that you have to surmount in day to day living all cause your thoughts to be haphazard and to be, what shall we say, a little bit dulled by the doom and gloom that is put out into the media for you to soak up. And then you begin to doubt your spirituality, your spiritual beliefs, and so that is why it is important that you come together to exchange your views, band together to sing your praises, to send your prayers out to us, because there is much that we can do with the energy that we can use, because, you know, the energy within your world can be quite harsh to us, the ambassadors of light that draw close to your earth vibration to bring you the help, the advice, the guidance that is there on offer to you.

The reading was quite a simple one, just each letter of the word being used to give you food for thought, so that you can understand how the spirit world works, how that spirit within you is so important, how we want you to be of service to God the Father by being helpful in your day to day work, so that you may, indeed, feel that you are doing God's work. That you are bringing forward the message that there is no death. Too many people think of your Spiritualism as maybe, to use a modern phrase, a cop out, so that you do not have to have a religion to follow; but you know, religion all over time has been, what shall we say, an excuse for man to have power over others to take control. The only thing that controls your world is God, the Great Spirit, the Creator of all life.

Look at your seasons: they change and evolve, and yet there are still seasons of summer, autumn, winter and spring. Because there is this life that will continue to breathe life into the physical world, to breathe life into the spiritual world also, and so it is your personal responsibility to take on your own thoughts, not to be overrun by negativity of the thought process, but to realise the positivity of the message within Spiritualism itself, within spirit itself; through eons of time the message has been given out about the spirit that you are here and now.

And so, we urge you to take up the challenge, because you are in control of your own thoughts and your own thought process. The problem is that if you are sensitive to the spirit world, then you are sensitive to others, and you can sometimes take on other people's responsibility, and so you have to learn that you must take responsibility for yourself, and in so doing be a pure channel for God the Father, for those in the spirit world that walk closely with you to guide, to help you, to uplift you, to give you strength when you have to face adversity, or adverse conditions.

And so, we would, indeed, tell to you that thoughts are indeed living things. Take control of your own mind, allow the spirit to grow within you. Allow spirituality to guide you forward and you cannot fail. Your life will be fulfilled, you will find peace, love, joy, harmony; all the things that you crave for in your world have to begin with you, the individual. We are not telling this to cause you dismay; we are telling this to bring about a positive change within you. That will help others to see that what you are saying about the spiritual reality of life is indeed the truth.

So, take on the challenge, my friends; go forward in life telling those that need your help all about the spirit world and the help that comes from God the Father, the Great Spirit. It is important to keep positive when all seems to be dark; you can shine the light of your own spirituality forward to dispel the darkness, to dispel the fear. There has been much written in many books from the Masters who have, through eons of time, come into the world of matter to show the way to all those that are willing to take up the challenge to develop their own spirituality and be channels for the spirit world. We welcome you all into the midst of that challenge to find out the truth about life and life eternal.

And so, we say to you, my friends, good night and God bless.